The Every Day God

40 Daily Devotions for Walking with God
through Everyday Moments

Misty Cramer

For more information, email mistycramer18@gmail.com.

ISBN: 979-8-88759-894-9 - paperback

ISBN: 979-8-88759-895-6 - ebook

Endorsements

If you'd like a jump-start to daily experiences in walking with God and applying biblical truth to those everyday experiences, read this book. Misty Cramer has done a masterful job describing poignant stories from her life. She finds the take-home principles that will enrich and deepen our Christian lives. These devotions make an ideal gift for any occasion.

Carol Kent, Founder & Director of Speak Up Ministries Speaker & Author of *He Holds My Hand: Experiencing God's Presence and Protection* (Tyndale)

The Every Day God devotional will lead you along a 40-day path of walking with Jesus through simple and relatable events of life. Misty draws deep spiritual truths from personal experiences, which are very relatable. We each have a unique journey with Jesus. This devotional will help draw you closer to God as you learn to reflect on the everyday events of your own life. You will be richer in spirit and grow in your love for Jesus as a result of this tender devotional.

Dyann Shepard, Author of *Wisdom Capturing the Power of Our Words*

Misty Cramer is a powerful storyteller. Her vulnerable personal stories, woven together with insightful biblical connections, are relatable and inspiring. *The Everyday God: 40 Daily Devotions for*

Walking with God through Everyday Moments will speak to your heart and soul. Each daily reading illuminates how God is present in our ordinary experiences and is always working to draw us closer to Him. This is such a refreshing and uplifting devotional for both new believers and those who have walked with God for a long time. If you need a daily dose of encouragement and a reminder of the Lord's love and faithfulness in your life, *The Everyday God* has my highest recommendation!

Laura Acuña, Speaker, Podcast Host, & Author of *Still Becoming: Hope, Help and Healing for the Diet-Weary Soul.*

Sometimes, we just need a friend who understands. Misty Cramer is that friend, and the words on these pages let you know you're not alone. Misty connects the dots from everyday experiences to the God who can guide you through those everyday experiences.

Jill Savage, Host of the No More Perfect Podcast & Author of 16 books, including *Real Moms…Real Jesus*

If Misty Cramer finds Gods presence and guidance in her every day experiences, so can you. Her candid honesty draws you in with emotion and expectancy. This 40-day devotional journey can help you discover God in your own every day moments. God sees you and reveals Himself to you daily in the midst of the little things.

Peg Arnold, Wonder of Women Ministry

Misty writes about the "Everyday God," the God Who shows up in all the chaos and messiness of life. She reminds us that God is with us through all the ups and downs of life. Her raw and honest writing will touch your heart, and her stories about finding God amid the chaos and messiness of life will give you hope. Whether you are going through trials or enjoying peace, this book will inspire you to seek God in your everyday life.

Andrea Lende, Bestselling Author of *Reading the Bible Cover to Cover in 365 Days*, Speaker, & Podcaster.

What type of mountain are you facing today? Life happens, and sometimes, every day is hard due to the weight of our circumstances. How do we climb mountains carrying heavy weights? Author Misty Cramer offers 40 days of encouragement to face your mountain with joy and Jesus as your daily guide through His Word. Join Misty on this climb. Discover the presence and power in your every day with our everyday God!

Christine Trimpe, Health Coach, Speaker, & Multi Award-Winning Author of Amazon Best-Seller *Seeking Joy through the Gospel of Luke: A Christmas to Calvary Advent Countdown*

DOWNLOAD YOUR FREE PRINTABLE GUIDE

5 Steps to Walking with God Through Everyday Moments

As a thank you for purchasing my book, I am giving you this free downloadable guide to encourage you to look for God in the everyday moments of your own life.

Download your copy today by going to:

MISTYCRAMER.COM

or scan

For daily encouragement, you can follow Misty at:

Facebook: Misty Cramer, Author & Speaker

Instagram: @mistydawncramer

To my best friend and husband, Todd

I would not have thought it possible for our love to be stronger with each passing day after thirty-nine years together. Yet, here we find ourselves, living out that truth. I am not naïve enough to think that happens on our own but only because we serve a loving and gracious God who continues to walk with us every step of the way. I praise Him daily for allowing me to be the one who does this journey alongside you. Your heart for me, our boys, and our ever-growing family is evident in all you do. Most importantly, your love for Jesus is what leads you each step of the way. For that reason, I will forever follow you anywhere, Todd, my Man. Thank you for your deep love for me and unwavering confidence in this book project. Thank you for Rummikub breaks when my brain could write no more and thank you for letting me win a few of those games too. I pray you enjoy turning the pages of this book as you soak in the many encounters with God we experienced on our journey together. I love you more than you know and look forward to seeing what's for us in the chapters ahead.

To my five sons, Stephen, Taylor, Zachary, Harrison, and Micah

You, my boys, have blessed me beyond what I can explain throughout the writing of this book. I had no idea I would have five cheerleaders who called, texted, visited, and checked-in on my writing in the ways the five of you did. While I chased my own dream of writing a book, each of you held my dream so closely to your own hearts as if it were your own. Your support has meant more than you will ever know. Thank you.

The majority of the words in this book are inspired by the days and years you lived under our roof. They were the days I poured into your lives, doing my best to shape five little boys into five Godly men. They were also the days each of you unknowingly poured into my soul. They were the days you taught me about love, laughter, and living life abundantly. I will hold those days tightly within my heart forever. I am so proud of the passionate, Jesus-loving men each of you have become. I love you so very much and hope you enjoy re-living pieces of your childhood through some of the stories that God used to shape each of our lives.

To Mom and Dad

I fail in my attempt to find words that will portray even a portion of the love and appreciation I have for both of you. You, my heroes, are selfless people who have given of yourselves in ways too innumerable to count. You are my friends, the people who support and encourage my family and I in ways that go beyond any expectations we may ever hold. You are my mom and dad, the people with whom I will always eagerly anticipate one more conversation in the "yellow room" and one more "time for a tea." I love you both.

To Grandma Zee, Grandma Cederberg, and Great-Aunt Marney

Your great zeal for life and the love for Jesus you held close to your hearts greatly shaped my life. The prayers you spoke for me while you were on this earth continue to reveal themselves in countless ways in my life. This book is one of those ways. Your lessons and stories live on in its pages and more importantly, in the lives of those of us who are still here.

To my grandchildren, Jada Marie, Layla Misty, and the many others I expect in the future. I pray you will enjoy these stories about a living God who taught us so much through the lives of your daddies. Always remember that Jesus loves you and that He will use every moment of every day to show you just how much.

To my Heavenly Father

To you, I give all the glory, honor, and praise for blessing me with a family who loves you and loves others so well. More importantly, I praise you for loving each of us enough to send your son, Jesus, to this earth to provide us with abundant life on earth and with eternal life when our time here is complete.

I love you, Jesus!

Hello to my new Friend and Reader,

As I sit at my kitchen table with two dogs at my feet, the rays of sunshine filter through the drapery and make their way across the table. The subtle sounds of springtime hang in the air. I close my eyes and envision you, my reader. I'm wondering if you are reading while out on your porch with a light breeze blowing through your hair and a cool drink in your hand. Maybe, instead, you are reading while snuggled on your couch under a blanket with a hot cup of coffee (or tea if you're like me) beside you. As my mind wonders, I am brought back to my writing. Regardless of the weather and regardless of your surroundings, I am thankful for you. I'm thankful you picked up this book. I pray you are prepared for a forty-day walk with Jesus as we explore how a magnificent God meets us even in the mundane portions of our lives.

As you read this book, my hope is that you will find yourself within its pages. The devotions are based on true stories from my life; however, I believe you will relate as you share in the similarities between my family and yours. My story includes laughter and love. It includes challenging moments as well as cherished ones. It includes times of growth and times of setbacks. My guess is your story does as well.

As tempting as it is for me to share details regarding the background of my childhood, marriage, and parenting in this note, I am going to refrain. As you turn the pages of this book, you will find those pieces of my story woven throughout the devotions. Each devotion begins with a scripture for the day. Following the scripture,

I share with you a story about the mundane happenings in my life. Yet, through each one, we will meet a magnificent God who makes them into something marvelous. After each story, there will be an application to your spiritual life, a time to pause for reflection, and a closing prayer.

Are you ready? Let's take this journey together. I have eagerly anticipated sharing with you pieces of my story and the journey I am on with God. Yet, my most profound prayer is that you will not only connect with me but more importantly, you will connect with the God who has each of our stories in His hands.

May God richly bless you as He shows up in your everyday moments.

Table of Contents

Introduction

As I laid on the couch watching the early morning sun slowly make its way through the curtains, I listened for any movement from around the house. Although I was far from being able to fall asleep, I laid there silent and still, prepared to close my eyes quickly if anyone should make a move to enter the room. If I could pretend I was asleep, this day wouldn't happen. My mom wouldn't need to share with my dad that I, their oldest, their eighteen-year-old, unmarried daughter, was pregnant.

Having told my mom the news first, we decided to wait to tell my dad until a doctor could confirm what I strongly suspected to be true. I'm certain it was the longest two weeks in my mom's marriage. The day had arrived for my dad to finally learn the news as I was, in fact, pregnant. During the conversation with Mom, I asked if she would tell Dad for me. As a way of compromise, we decided I would come home from college that night to be at home when she told him. So, there I was on the couch, pretending to be asleep and waiting for that conversation to happen.

I could hear the sounds of my parents waking up and making their way to the kitchen. Keeping my eyes closed tightly, I heard their footsteps make their way across the carpet and into the kitchen. The noise of the coffee maker started. Soon, the smell made its way to the living room where I continued to lay, hoping to be invisible. After the coffee was poured, the footsteps stopped at the table. The typical morning chatter between them quickly went from normal tones to a hushed murmur. My heart beat wildly as I anticipated the words my mom spoke making their way into my dad's heart, piercing it. His little girl was not who he thought she was. She wasn't living up to the expectations he had for her. He could not be proud of her. She was flawed and soon to be very visibly flawed.

I tightened my eyes as I heard footsteps again. The single set of footsteps I recognized as my dad's were making their way towards me. I could hear those steps leaving the kitchen and stepping onto the carpet. They were now in the living room. *Please Lord,* I thought, *can't I just disappear? Can't I take away the pain that I've brought on this family? The embarrassment? Can't I have a redo?*

Holding my tears and my breath in, I felt his body sit down on the couch where I was laying. It would no longer do any good to pretend I was sleeping. I sat up slowly, opened my eyes, and grimaced at the thought of what I was sure to find in my dad's eyes. I was wholly unprepared for what was actually there. I stared into the eyes of a man whose own eyes were not only filled with tears but with so much more. He held a box of Kleenex in his hand and said, "Mom said we may need these." He reached over and enveloped me in his arms. We cried together.

I don't remember any other words being spoken during that time. However, I do remember that what I saw in his eyes were three things I didn't even realize I longed to see. Love. Forgiveness. Acceptance. The man I needed the most in that moment to love, forgive, and accept me did exactly that. And those things washed over me in a way I didn't fully understand yet needed so badly.

We all have similar stories, don't we? Some parts of our stories are exhilarating and exciting. Other parts are heavy and hard. Our lives are a combination of all the above. If we look closely enough, we see God show up and meet us in these stories in ways that leave us different. You will find many such stories throughout this devotion. Some are ones from my childhood while others are stories I've experienced as a parent. The common thread in each of them is they are simply everyday experiences. They are experiences that you, too, may have walked through. They are experiences God shed His light upon in such a way to teach me something about His character.

God desires to teach us in the midst of every situation. We only need to be awakened to His spirit. The Every Day God is based upon that truth. It is a book that contains everyday situations we can all relate to in some form. Each situation shines with God's light and a desired lesson.

So often, we go about our daily circumstances without considering how the circumstance connects us to God. Whether we are at a chaotic stage of life with jobs and children or a quieter stage that may sometimes seem too quiet, we often struggle to acknowledge God in our midst. We may not consider what He wants to teach us right there in our chaos or there in our quietness.

It is while considering those thoughts I determined to seek God in the middle of these everyday circumstances. I soon found a lesson about forgiveness shining through when my son forgave his brother after his finger got slammed in a van door. A lesson about grace was brought to mind as I dealt with the messiness of a box of cereal being emptied on the living room floor. A lesson about setting time aside for Jesus confronted me when my son sought intentional time with me at the end of a busy day. The lessons began to abound, shining brightly from the simple everyday moments of my life.

Choose today to begin this 40-day journey to see what lessons God has for you in the midst of your everyday situations. May we move forward with the God who desires time with us every day as we walk hand-in-hand with Him through our everyday moments.

Day 1

The Unshakable Voice

And the peace of God, which transcends all understanding, will guard
your hearts and your minds in Christ Jesus.

Philippians 4:7

After the bedroom lights had been turned off, the darkness would consume me all too quickly and make me believe the most eerie things were out to get me. This was not the case every night, but it did happen fairly often. Sometimes, I would lay there wide-awake, making monsters out of the clothing I had thrown over the chair earlier in the day. Other times, I would refuse to hang my leg over the edge of the top bunk for fear someone or something would grab it and pull me to the floor. I'm not sure who was going to grab it, but I knew it wasn't going to be good. On really scary nights, I would gaze out the window, listen to the wind blow, and watch the trees. Their branches seemingly jumped to life, reached over the roof, and clawed at my window, begging to come inside.

Thankfully, those times were usually interrupted by a familiar voice - the deep, commanding yet comforting voice I had come to know as my dad's. I would close my eyes and hear his voice downstairs as he walked through the kitchen to grab one more snack before he went to bed. Although I couldn't make out the conversation, I listened to him and my mom speak. My heart was calmed simply by hearing their voices. I was comforted. I was able to peacefully close my eyes and slowly fall asleep. I was safe from the monsters. Safe from being pulled off my bed and onto the floor. Safe from branches that threatened to reach in my window and take me. My dad's voice provided me with the peace and comfort I needed at that very moment when I was convinced darkness would devour me.

As adults, the darkness is a bit more real than the clothing monster or the branches we are certain are attempting to reach into our windows. This darkness is probably more terrifying because we are more easily consumed by it. Like my childhood terrors, it comes in various forms. It could be a health scare for yourself or a family member. It may come in the form of a marriage falling apart. It could be that never-ending, every-growing pile of bills on the table. It sometimes comes in the form of regret - regret of things unsaid or words spoken in haste. It sneaks its way into our minds in the form of uncertainty - uncertainty about the future for our children, or perhaps, for ourselves. Darkness is so creative and limitless because it takes the form of our deepest fears, scaring us even more than those childhood fears that fought for our attention.

Although we are unable to hear the voices that may have comforted us as children, there is a voice we can always hear. Our Savior provides a voice that has the ability to break through the darkest of moments. His voice is able to remind us that in the midst of health scares, failing relationships, regret, and uncertainty, He is present. His voice assures us that nothing that happens is a surprise to Him. His voice overwhelms us with peace and comfort in a world where darkness still wants to devour us.

If you are feeling scared, uncertain, filled with regret, or perhaps, fearful of the dark, I pray the Lord Jesus comes upon you right this minute and speaks clearly to your heart, reminding you that He's got you. His voice is the light you need in your darkness.

Ponder & Pray

What words of assurance do you need the Lord to speak to you today?

_____

_____

_____

_____

Lord Jesus, sometimes, the darkness tries to overtake me. It doesn't look the same as it did when I was a child, but it is scary, all the same. I ask that you open my ears to hear the words of comfort that you have to offer me during the times when I feel the darkness making its way into my heart. I know I can trust you with my fears and my darkest times. Amen.

Day 2

Offering from a Child

For if the willingness is there, the gift is acceptable according to what one has, not according to what one does not have.

2 Corinthians 8:12

As a mom of five sons, we had some very interesting Sunday morning church services. To say my husband and I were unable to listen intently during the worship services would be an understatement. Some Sundays, there were more trips back and forth to the nursery or time spent "sshhing" than there was focusing on the worship. However, we remained diligent in attending each Sunday. It proved, more often than not, to be very worthwhile for a variety of reasons. On one particular Sunday, the lesson God taught me arrived not through the sermon but through my six-year-old son.

Our family was all settled into the pew or as settled as you get a family of seven. I was doing my usual, "Ok guys, it's time to quiet down. The service is about to start." Apparently, my son was not real thrilled with my notice. Tapping his grandma on the leg, he inquired, "Grandma, is it only the preacher who gets to talk loud on Sundays?"

I didn't get to hear Grandma's answer, but it seemed to satisfy him. That was until the next question came to his mind. Tap. Tap. I felt his little hand on my shoulder. His neck craned toward me. As I lowered my head to him, he cupped his hand around my ear and whispered, "Mom, is money the only thing we can give Jesus as an offering?"

Wow…great question, I thought. So, I leaned over and began to explain to him that there were many things we could offer up to Jesus. As I began to explain some of those things, it was apparent that he already had something in mind. He quickly grabbed one of the extra offering envelopes from the pew in front of us. I wondered what he brought to church that he was going to place in this little envelope.

Instead, I watched as he carefully and quietly pulled the envelope apart by separating each side that had been glued together. Soon, it was one small, flat piece of paper. He laid it on the hymnal and began smoothing it with his hand as one would if they were ironing a delicate piece of fabric.

Minutes later, he had a pencil in his hand. He drew right up until the offering plate made its way down our pew. As he saw it approaching, he quickly took his envelope and folded it back up precisely the way he found it. He finished the last fold just in time to place it in the plate as it passed in front of him.

A smile passed between us. I could see the sparkle of satisfaction in his eyes for putting his offering into the plate.

After church, I made my way back to the ushers. They knew immediately why I had come into the room. They had the little offering envelope already opened and laying on the table next to the money they had been counting.

Ah, yes. They had found his gift to Jesus and planned to post it on the bulletin board in the church narthex for all to see. Having not seen it yet, I asked them if I could look at it. As I held the envelope, I looked down to see a detailed picture of Jesus hanging on the cross with arms stretched wide, thorn crown on his head, and nails in his hands and feet.

My son had figured out how to give an offering to the Lord that day. He didn't have money, but he found a pencil. He didn't have an art pad, but he found an offering envelope. He had the heart to offer a gift to Jesus using whatever means he could at that moment in time. For my son, it meant drawing a picture for Jesus.

As I looked at that picture, I thought about the many ways we can offer ourselves to Jesus. I considered the scripture that teaches us that giving comes from our hearts.

Romans 12:1 says, "Present your bodies as a living sacrifice, holy and acceptable to God, which is your spiritual worship." It's about our hearts. It's about allowing God to make us clean so we can give ourselves as a holy and acceptable sacrifice to him. It's about surrendering to

Him so He can use us as He desires. Second Corinthians 9:7 says, "Each one must give as he has decided in his heart, not reluctantly or under compulsion, for God loves a cheerful giver." Again, it's about our heart. It's about aligning ourselves with Him.

What is it today that we can give to Jesus? Is it allowing Him to use us to call a neighbor who has been struggling? You know, the one you avoid calling because you know it will be an hour-long phone call. Maybe, it's time for that hour long phone call. Is it taking a meal to the family who has been struggling? It could be for the single parent who is barely keeping his or her head up between work and the children's needs. You may not realize how much of a relief it would be for this parent to not have to cook for a night. Is it sending some money to a person who has been on your heart? Maybe they need a night out with their spouse? Maybe they need money for groceries?

The list of ideas is endless. We can offer ourselves to our Heavenly Father in so many ways through the serving of His people. Remember when He said, "What you do for the least of these, you do unto me." How great to think that when we serve these people with our hearts aligned with the Father, we are actually serving the Father.

We are giving our offering to Him. We are placing our envelope, whatever that looks like, in the offering plate and laying it at His feet. For my son, it was in the form of a drawing of His Savior. In what form will your offering be given?

What will you give to Jesus today?

_____

_____

_____

_____

Heavenly Father, you have blessed me with so much more than I could ever deserve. I come to you today with a desire to give back to you. I want to offer you my finances, consistently giving to you back a portion of what you have blessed me with. I want to offer you my time; please direct me in the ways you desire for me to spend it. I want to offer you the gifts and talents you have given me; guide me in how to use them to serve you more fully. Create in me a clean heart as I offer myself to you as a living sacrifice for your service. Amen.

Day 3

Quitting Isn't an Option

May the God who gives endurance and encouragement give you the
same attitude of mind toward each other that Christ Jesus had.

Romans 15:5

The sun weaved its way through the trees and rested in the stillness of the Kentucky mountain side. More than twenty energetic high school students surrounded me. Their eager excitement sent a buzz of energy through the air. We were impatient to make it up the mountain to experience a view that would be unlike anything we see in our rural Michigan neighborhood. The students took off down the path with joyous laughter. Light shoving and racing ensued as they enthusiastically tried to pass one another along the way. Quick stops for drinks would have them pause momentarily to take in their surroundings, from the winding path ahead to the trees towering above to the rock ledges on either side. The pauses didn't last long. Though they couldn't see the end of the path and the top of the mountain was still a far way off, they pressed on in anticipation of the view.

The minutes soon became hours. The spread between students grew larger. Some could be heard far up the path while others at the end of the line struggled to keep going. Sweat poured down our faces. The scrapes on our arms and legs were too innumerable to count. Every so often, a voice from the front of the pack would yell, "Come on you guys! You got this! Let's go!" The voice would quickly trail off as the person turned to continue the journey.

The space between myself and the people in front continued to grow exponentially. Occasionally, I came across a couple students resting on the side of the path. After a few words and another quick drink, their young legs would take off as they rushed to catch the rest of the pack.

With the second hour now ticking away, my body was weary. I was several decades older than these students and was also dealing with some health issues. These health issues not only physically held me back but frustrated my formerly determined mind and healthy body. As my legs trembled from fatigue and my body succumbed to the exhaustion, I realized this was not the day I was going to climb this mountain. In fact, I was not going to go even one step further. I encouraged the students who had hung back with me to keep going and take lots of pictures of the view. Reluctantly, they set off without me towards the prize, the top of that mountain. Struggling to make peace with my decision, I settled down against a tree. I would reconnect with the group upon their descent.

After a few minutes, I could hear a voice yelling my name. I couldn't see anyone at first, but I heard the sounds of rock, dirt, and shoes sliding down the mountain.

"Misty, you're coming with us!"

I looked up to see one of my students hurrying towards me. He had been leading the crew, certainly positioned to be the first one to make it to the top. Yet, here he was, now standing before me.

"We're not doing the mountain without you, Misty. Let's go!"

Apparently, the news that I was going to wait and catch the students on their way back down the mountain had made its way through the group. Before I could argue or offer an explanation, he lifted me off the ground, put me on his back, and started hiking up the mountain.

Not knowing if I should laugh or cry, I finally convinced him to set me back down. He only agreed as long as I promised to continue the climb with him at my side. Soon, there were others yelling down the mountain, "Is she coming?"

"Yup! I got her!"

With that, we all continued on our journey. The voices of support and encouragement could be heard until the end. They offered to carry me throughout the climb, but I declined, my energy now renewed. This young man's steady voice offered reassurance as I took each step, telling me that I could, and would, accomplish this challenge.

It is not news to you when I say life is full of mountains and challenges seemingly too big to conquer. Oh, they may not come in the form of a physical mountain that delivers sweat and scrapes upon our attempts to climb, but we experience such challenges all the same. Perhaps it's in the form of the sweat of anxiety as we struggle to put our marriage back together again. Maybe it takes shape as scrapes on our heart from the harsh words spoken by a friend. Our mountain may include fatigue from the day-in, day-out routine that sneeringly taunts, "Is this all there is?"

I did make it to the top of the mountain that hot afternoon. I was able to soak in the breathtaking view overlooking the mountain range. Yet, that wasn't the most spectacular view that day. The most spectacular view was the one of this high school student who, surrounded by his peers, had just exemplified the beauty of humanity by offering support and sacrificing self for his youth leader. That is the view God desires to present to us.

There are mountains to climb, my friend. However, you do not need to resign yourself by saying, "This is not the day I'm going to make it up this mountain." You have the promise of our Lord who will make the journey with you. His desire is for you to come to Him when you are too weary for the travel. His desire is for you to allow Him to pour into you. Sometimes, that is through other people He places in your life. Other times, it may be through a peace He gives you during your prayer time or a scripture He lays on your heart. Regardless of how He chooses to get you up the mountain, His goal is to get you there, even if it means carrying you on His back.

Perhaps you are someone who is doing well today. Maybe you have already conquered some mountains. Now, God is asking you to help someone else with their difficult climb. Ask the Lord today who needs some assistance for the climb. I know you will find the view at the top so much sweeter when you are able to stand with the one you helped along the way.

Ponder & Pray

What type of mountain are you facing today?
What could you do to assist someone else who is climbing a challenging mountain today?

_____

_____

_____

_____

Heavenly Father, life is hard sometimes. Often, we have mountains to climb that seem insurmountable. They look too big. We are tired. We don't know how to move forward. During those times, we acknowledge it is no accident when you provide us with others who give us a call, pray for us, bring us a meal, send a card, or literally walk hand-in-hand beside us. Thank you for those people. And Lord, I ask today, if there is someone who needs me to walk along side of them, direct me to them, bring their name to my heart right now, and allow me the opportunity to support them. Amen.

Day 4

The Good Medicine

Our mouths were filled with laughter, our tongues with songs of joy.

Psalm 126:2

I remember her coming to the birthday party. Every time we had a birthday party for one of the boys, my grandma and she made the trip over. This time was different though. This time, a tear made its way down my cheek as she walked through our door. This time, she walked into our home without my grandma. Her sister had died just months before, and for the first time, she arrived without her best friend.

It was hard for me not to have my grandma there, but I knew it was even harder for my great aunt to be here without her. With both of their husbands in heaven, these two had become almost inseparable. They met for lunches. They took trips to special towns around the area and enjoyed visits with their children. And yes, they attended birthday parties together.

As I sat down at the table with my Great Aunt Marney, we began talking about Grandma. It was during that time of sharing she said something that has always stuck with me. I asked her what she missed the most about her times with Grandma. The biggest smile came across her face as she said, "Laughing." Really, laughing? I thought about these two sisters, best friends, and was intrigued to find out more about their laughing. I mean, I knew they always had smiles on their faces when I saw them. They were obviously "filled with the joy of the Lord." However, I had to further investigate; I wanted what they had.

As the smile continued to spread across her face, I caught a glimpse of liquid in her eyes. Tears filled her eyes as she told me more about laughing with her sister. She told me how they would start talking and would finish each other's sentences. If one of them laughed, it was sure to make the other laugh as if laughing was the most contagious thing on the planet. They would giggle and laugh with one another about nothing in particular until their "bellies ached."

"I miss laughing with my sister," she said. Her eyes looked beyond the walls of the house as she envisioned times when she sat at the kitchen table, finishing her sister's sentences, and laughing until their bellies ached.

Laughter is one of those things that truly can make us feel better. Its positive impacts can be felt in both our physical and emotional health. It's a stress reliever. It fights depression. It lowers blood pressure. All of that shouldn't come as a surprise, however, since scripture tells us, "[a] cheerful heart is good medicine" (Proverbs 17:22). What a gift God has given us in laughter!

Let us make this the day to laugh. We can do this! Can you remember when you last laughed the type of laugh that couldn't be contained? Or laughed the contagious laughter of my grandma and Great Aunt Marney? It's beneficial for us. It will make our day brighter. I encourage you today, and every day, to find a way to laugh. Find those people who bring it out in you. Let out a laughter that allows God to infuse you with His joy and laugh the contagious, belly-aching laughter of my grandma and Great Aunt Marney.

Ponder & Pray

What could you do today that will bring laughter and joy into your day and someone else's day?

_____

_____

_____

_____

Heavenly Father, your word says laughter is good for us, good for our souls, and good for our bodies. I desire to experience the type of laughter that brings joy to every part of my being. Allow me to experience that laughter today. And perhaps, you could also bring someone into my life today that we might experience that joy-filled laughter together. Amen.

Day 5

Hope for the Heart

May the God of hope fill you with all joy and peace as you trust in him,
so that you may overflow with hope by the power of the Holy Spirit.

Romans 15:13

Our phone was one of the heavy black ones. It wasn't connected to the wall. Instead, it sat on a shelf, atop a pile of Yellow Pages. (Some of you younger readers may have to ask someone what the Yellow Pages were. ☺) Although the phone was clunky, I felt lucky to have one with a really long cord attached to it. That meant I could carry (barely) the thing across the room and relocate to a place where I would have a little more privacy.

I was waiting for a phone call from my biological dad. You see, I lived with my mom and my dad. The dad I lived with was the man who married my mom. He also was the man who took care of me, loved me, and taught me. He was the kind of dad in every little girl's dream. Therefore, he was Dad. This meant the person I was waiting on was my biological dad. It was a complicated relationship at best. However, to the little girl who was waiting for the phone call, it seemed pretty simple. When you say you're going to call, call. And so, I waited. I watched the clock eager to hear that…..

Finally, my ears perked up, my chin lifted, and something resembling a smile even came across my face. The phone was finally ringing! Yes!

I lifted the phone off the shelf and lugged it across the room. I opened the dining room door, walked out to the entry way, went down a couple steps, and sat down on the floor. The call from Daddy finally came, and I was going to be in the best spot possible. I had so much to tell him. I needed a place with the least number of distractions. The floor in the entryway seemed close to perfect.

"Hi Daddy!"

Hmmm. Daddy's response was not what I expected. In fact, I wondered if there was something wrong with the phone. I couldn't understand what he was saying. I had come out to the entryway, so my brother and sisters wouldn't bother me and the radio wouldn't interfere. This was supposed to be the spot where I could hear him clearly. I had executed my plan of privacy perfectly. Why wasn't it working?

"What Daddy? I don't understand what you're saying."

Noise came from the other end of the line, but I could not make out the words, or rather, the mumbling.

"Daddy?" It didn't take long for my young heart to figure out that Daddy wasn't quite right tonight. Mom knowingly looked down at me from the top of the steps. She sadly took the phone from me and went back into the house with it. I'm not sure what words were said between them, but I had quickly learned what a drunk daddy sounded like that night.

I'd like to say that was the only time I was disappointed by this type of behavior, but my sister and I had become accustomed to disappointment from our biological dad. Whether it was from phone calls like that one or not showing up when it was time to pick us up for visitations, it became a normal part of how our relationship developed.

We all have our stories of disappointment, pain, and rejection. Maybe like me, it's by a parent who wasn't there when you needed him or her. Perhaps a spouse has left you with a gaping hole in your heart. Maybe a child has turned away from you and God, rejecting the values you hold dear to your heart. Possibly the church has brought you pain, leaving you lonely and questioning God. Unfortunately, the list of possibilities is endless, but I'm so thankful we don't have to allow disappointment, pain, and rejection to remain in us.

We serve a God who is in the business of healing hearts. The condition of your heart is so very important to Him. He desires to provide you with hope right now in the midst of your situation. He desires to mend the broken pieces within your heart. He will begin to stich those holes in your heart, even the ones you think are too deep for anyone to reach. My prayer for you today is that you would allow Him to reach deeply into your heart to replace disappointment with contentment, pain with healing, and rejection with acceptance.

Will you acknowledge a pain you have in your heart today? Will you allow God to reach in and heal it for you today?

_____

_____

_____

_____

Heavenly Father, you know the depths of my soul and the deepest portions of my heart. You know the pieces of me that are broken and in need of healing. I ask that you examine this broken heart of mine. Examine the parts that seem to overwhelm me with pain. Explore the parts I choose to hide from even myself. Place your healing hand upon me. Mend my brokenness and fill me with all the good and perfect things that come only from you. Amen.

Day 6

Know the Gatekeeper

The gatekeeper opens the gate for him, and the sheep listen to his voice.
He calls his own sheep by name and leads them out.

John 10:3

As our sons ran to the entry of Deer Acres, their hearts pounded with excitement for what the day ahead would hold. Deer Acres, a Storybook Park, was created and owned by my grandparents. They paused briefly at the ticket counter to say hello to my uncle before quickly running into the arms of Grandma, who sat on a nearby bench. They could hardly contain themselves. They knew these hugs were important; but boy, there was a park out there to explore, and they were ready.

My uncle and grandma understood this dilemma. With a wave of their hands, they encouraged the boys to get on with their adventures. All of us knew the day would end right back at this location with one final stop, the cherished Souvenir Shop. It was sure to hold some type of treasure that each boy could not live without.

The race down the path ensued. The older boys ran on ahead while the younger boys tried to keep up. Baby brother sat in the stroller soaking in the unfamiliar sights and sounds. We went straight to the monkey exhibit. Laughter filled the air as they pointed at the mischievous monkeys. The monkeys did not hold their attention for long, however. Off they darted down the path to the peacocks. After admiring their fanning feathers, we found ourselves at the rides. Here, they would not only experience the gorilla chasing them on the safari (a costume gorilla that seemed pretty darn real to little boys), but they would get to drive their own Model T cars around the track.

The day continued with feeding the deer and goats, stopping by the alligator exhibit to see if it would move, and pausing to eat cotton candy. Days at Deer Acres always seemed like they should go on forever. As a mom, I was thankful that sentiment continued from my childhood to my own children.

It soon was evident that for us to have time to go to Grandma's house before we headed home, we would need to wrap up our day at the park. This would have been difficult except the boys all knew they would be given the opportunity to purchase something from the Souvenir Shop before we left. By purchase I mean the boys would pick something out and hand my aunt and uncle some of the meager change they had to spend. It would somehow be just enough to pay for their special item.

On this particular day, one of my sons chose toy handcuffs. They seemed pretty official; they came with a key and were made of metal. He proudly left the store with these handcuffs, and we all made our way to Grandma's for a short visit before heading home. During the two-minute trip from the park to Grandma's, our son not only put on his handcuffs but also lost the attached key.

"Grandma, I am trapped. I lost my key!" he said with more frustration than fear as we entered Grandma's house.

Fully confident Grandma would figure out a solution to his problem, he put out his hands for her to examine the situation. His small hands were indeed trapped, and she saw no way to break him free. However, that did not stop Grandma. After a few moments, Grandma made the magic happen. She did what only Grandma could do. She picked up the phone and called the Souvenir Shop. Before we knew it, an employee was at her door with another set of keys for the handcuffs. With that, our little guy was set free!

Just as Grandma was the gatekeeper for my son, we also have a gatekeeper. It's important to know our gatekeeper. He is the one who holds the keys and who can provide freedom. Our son's lack of concern about being trapped in his handcuffs was proof that he trusted the one who held the keys. He knew Grandma would figure out a way to set him free. And she did do just that.

We have the opportunity to have a relationship with our gatekeeper, God Himself, through His Son, Jesus. Our trust in Him is even more sure and secure than my son's trust in Grandma because God is perfect and incapable of leaving us trapped when we fully surrender to Him. What a gift that is to us! Can you imagine a relationship with the Creator of the world? That should get us excited. That should bring us more joy than what my sons were experiencing when they walked in the park that day. That should bring us more joy than my son running into Grandma's house, knowing she could set him free. (And that's a lot of joy!)

As you go about your day today, take some time to evaluate your life. Take a moment to assess if you are trusting the One who holds the keys. I pray you will trust in the gatekeeper to set you free from the worries of the day and from any sin that has you tightly bound. Trust Him to set you free from the crazy schedule that saps your time and energy from His priorities. Most importantly, embrace His freedom because it is important to have a relationship with the One who holds the keys.

Ponder & Pray

What sin, worry, or fear will you give to the Lord, your Gatekeeper, today? In return, ask the Lord what freedom He desires to give you in place of that sin, worry, or fear.

_____

_____

_____

_____

Heavenly Father, I thank you for holding the keys. I thank you for being the gatekeeper. I thank you that I can trust you to set me free. Would you bring to my mind, right now, anything in my heart that needs to be released to you? I give you this, Lord. Take it from me and give me the full confidence that I can trust in you. I know you not only will take it, but you will replace it with your Spirit. I thank you and praise you for allowing me the opportunity to have a relationship with the One who holds the keys. Amen.

Day 7

Hidden Within

But the Lord said to Samuel, "Do not consider his appearance or his height, for I have rejected him. The Lord does not look at the things people look at. People look at the outward appearance, but the Lord looks at the heart."

1 Samuel 16:7

The voices of my three youngest boys began to escalate as their civil discussion over which movie to watch turned into an argument. The vote was at a standstill. Two of the boys insisted on *The Black Stallion* while the other was holding to his conviction that *Runaway Ralph* was the sure choice for the evening.

After a bit more back-and-forth, the brother fighting for *Runaway Ralph* relinquished his vote and volunteered to go downstairs to bring the movie upstairs. My son's response puzzled me. I thought it a bit strange that the "loser" was now volunteering to bring the movie. I'd like to say that this was one of those times when my good parenting came into play. Perhaps he was choosing to be a good "loser" and made the choice to do a little something nice for his brothers. However, the gleam in his eye made me realize this was definitely not one of those moments.

I watched him smirk as he ran downstairs to grab the movie. He brought it back, handed it to them, and walked into the kitchen eagerly taking the seat next to me. He proceeded to watch his brothers take the movie from its case and place it in the machine. In fact, he watched this as if he were watching the most captivating movie plot unfold right before his seven-year-old eyes.

"Son," I asked suspiciously, "what exactly is going on? Aren't you going to watch the movie with them?"

Between laughs, he leaned over to my ear and whispered, "I put the movie I wanted to watch in the movie case of the one they wanted to watch! I tricked them!"

At about the same time, his brothers figured out they had been handed the correct movie case but with the wrong movie tucked inside it. His trick was met with a yell from the other room. "Hey! This isn't our movie! Mom!"

The expression on his face as his brothers figured out his trick said it all; he greatly enjoyed watching his plan unfold.

When I think back on his little trick, it makes me wonder how often we display a movie cover that isn't representative of how we are feeling inside. Perhaps the outside says, *The*

Black Stallion, but the inside shows *Runaway Ralph*. Reality is quickly exposed when we hit the play button.

I often wonder why we feel the great need to hide ourselves and the persistent struggles we have on our journey. I wonder why we convince ourselves that no one would approve of us if they could see what was really under our cover. I wonder why we listen to the lies that tell us we are not good enough. I question the legitimacy of wearing a cover in order to protect ourselves from those we assume are looking down upon us.

We imagine if someone knew about our marriage problems, they would be horrified. If they knew we had a child who we haven't spoken to for years, they would shamefully shake their heads at us. We think if they knew how in debt we were, they would judge us. We imagine them pointing their fingers as we become the center of their gossip circles.

So, we hide our tears behind forced smiles. We strategically position insecurities behind walls of fraudulent confidence. We inaccurately assume that if anyone knew the truth about us, they would uncover our deeply concealed secret: we simply are not good enough. Not good enough to be friends with them. Not good enough to be a part of the church. Not good enough to have our children join in playdates. Simply, not good enough for God.

Oh, my dear friend, am I touching any cords here? This thinking is so far from what God has intended for us. This isn't at all how He created us to exist. He calls us to be real, to love ourselves the way He loves us. He reminds us throughout scripture that He created us and is pleased with His creation.

I'm not saying it's easy to unveil the real person under the cover. I'm not even saying it's important to share your struggles with everyone. However, I am saying there is freedom in pressing that play button for those we trust. There's assurance from a God who loves us. There's a peace that will come along with accepting one another and loving one another.

I pray that when the opportunity comes for you to unveil the real you today, you will be bold in doing so. For when you take that step at being authentic, you will give others the permission to do the same. Soon, you will find yourself in a healthy relationship in which you can truly walk with one another and encourage one another on this often-difficult journey of life.

Ponder & Pray

What part of your life is difficult for you to share with God and others?

_____

_____

_____

_____

Heavenly Father, I am sorry for the way I not only hide from other people but also for my attempts to hide from you. My desire is to be thankful for the way you have created me by embracing all those crazy pieces of me that I often want to bury. Please examine my heart today and unveil those parts of me I attempt to hide. Give me boldness to share my authentic self with others as well. Amen.

Day 8

Grab the Hammer

. . . being confident of this, that he who began a good work in you will carry it on to completion until the day of Christ Jesus.

Philippians 1:6

Saturday was finally here! As a twelve-year-old child, I always looked forward to Saturdays. It meant no alarm would wake me up for school. My day would hold more flexibility; the possibilities were endless. My sister, brother, and I could go outside to work on the fort we were creating in the backyard. Perhaps mom would make a big meal and even bake a delicious treat for us. Yes, it was finally Saturday, and I knew it was going to be a good day.

Not soon after I made my way downstairs from my bedroom, my dad asked me to meet him out in the barn. Now, one might think this would throw a wrench in the

Saturday I had envisioned, but I actually loved hanging out with Dad in the barn. He had a way of making me feel like I was useful; he had a way of making me feel as if I was needed as I worked alongside him. So, eager to see what he had in mind for me, I scarfed down my breakfast and headed for the barn.

When Dad saw me coming, he went over to his workbench. He grabbed a hammer, some nails, and some signs and put them all in a bag. *What in the world would those items have to do with me,* I wondered. Reading my body language and facial expression, Dad grabbed one of the signs out of the bag. It was a small, brightly painted, orange sign that simply read "NO HUNTING." Still unsure of what this sign had to do with me, I eagerly waited for him to explain.

"Misty, I need you to ride your bike over to that field," he continued as he pointed down the road. "Stop at each one of the telephone poles, reach as high as you can, and put a sign in each post."

With that said, he smiled, handed me the bag, and went back into the barn. *Wow,* I thought, *this is a big job. This is a big responsibility. This is a big deal because this is something my dad trusts me to do without any help.* My excitement momentarily turned to anxiety. *Am I really old enough to do this on my own? Can I reach high enough up the pole? What if my skinny arms don't have enough muscle to pound the nails into the poles?*

A bit nervous for the job ahead, I got on my banana seat bike and wrapped the bag full of my "tools" around the ape hanger handlebars. I peddled off as if I had just been given a secret mission to save the world.

Many years later and even into adulthood, I would drive by that field and notice some of those signs were still posted. There they hung exactly the height that this twelve-year-old could reach while stretching up on her tippy toes. The words had faded some. The nails were rusty. The orange was no longer shining brightly. Yet, the feelings of what that day held for me were still tucked deep within my heart. I am forever thankful for a dad who gave me the opportunity to accomplish a job that I believed far exceeded my ability. Though he provided me with the bag of tools to success-fully complete the job, he provided me with something more: trust. He trusted because he had equipped his little girl with everything she needed to be successful on this mission. It was this unseen tool that made her realize that if he believed she would be successful, then she, indeed, would be successful.

Have you ever been given an assignment by someone and doubted that you were equipped to accomplish it? Has the trust that someone placed in you helped you realize that yes, you really could accomplish that assignment?

I think God often does this very thing to us. When He does, I am reminded of my twelve-year-old self who was given the assignment of hanging the signs. At first, I hear God's job and am excited about what it might involve. It could be one of my speaking engagements, teaching a bible study, or visiting someone He has in mind. Sure God, that sounds great! I mean, after all, it is the God of the universe requesting I join Him in a project. How cool is that! My excitement is quickly tempered by questioning whether I am equipped for the job. *Really God? You want me to do. . . what? What qualifications do I have? Why would you choose me? I don't even know that person.*

Have you ever felt called by God to do a job that you felt unqualified to accomplish? One of the wonderful things about God is that He does intentionally ask us to accomplish jobs we feel insecure about or unequipped to handle. Why would a loving God do such a thing? Reliance. It allows us the opportunity to walk closely with Him and be dependent upon Him to complete the assignment. After all, if we can do it on our own, we usually will leave Him out of the process. So, if He has called you to do something that seems too big for you, celebrate! Because regardless of what it is He is requesting, He promises you can trust Him. He who has called you to a job, also fully believes you are equipped by Him to carry out the mission.

Ponder & Pray

Has God asked you to do something you don't feel equipped to do? Are you willing to trust Him as you move forward with the assignment?

_____

_____

_____

_____

Heavenly Father, I will admit that sometimes I get anxious and nervous and even question whether I am qualified for the calling you have placed on my life. However, today, I lay aside any anxiety and nervousness. I ask that you replace it with trust. I am ready to step forward into your plans, trusting that you have prepared me for everything you have asked of me. Amen.

Day 9

Talk Time

*You are my hiding place; you will protect me from trouble and surround
me with songs of deliverance. I will instruct you and teach you in the
way you should go; I will counsel you with my loving eye on you.*

Psalm 32:7-8

Bedtime used to be the part of the day we eagerly anticipated as we gathered our sons for their snacks and
family prayers before tucking them for the night. However,
bedtime had recently transitioned into a time of tears and
frustration. One of our sons suddenly was having a difficult
time. At eight years old, he would anxiously get up from
his bed, frustrated because sleep eluded him. This went on
for some time. As a result, my husband and I grew more
tense as bedtime approached each day.

After talking the situation over with my husband, we decided to implement "talk time" before putting our son to bed. "Talk time" would consist of intentional one-on-one conversation between my husband and our son. So, the next evening after our family prayers, my husband scooped up our son and placed him on his lap in the big chair in the corner of the living room while I finished tucking the rest of the boys into bed. They talked about their day, but the conversation mainly centered around the little Spiderman toy that happened to be in our son's hand. After about ten minutes, my husband gave our son a goodnight hug and kiss. He promised to continue "talk time" the following night. Our son jumped out of Daddy's arms with a smile on his face and went to bed.

The next day, our son mentioned to me that Daddy liked talking about his toys with him. So, he spent much of the day considering which toy he would take for his "talk time."

"I'm picking Godzilla for tonight, Mom!" he said, beaming as he held up his Godzilla toy. He set it aside in anticipation for the evening discussion. This pattern continued for days. Although the toys he chose varied, his excitement never faded.

One night, our little guy noticed it was getting late, and Daddy wasn't home yet. I reminded our son that Daddy had a church meeting, but he would be sure to have "talk time" as soon as he got home. Relief spread across his face as it sunk into his heart that his daddy had not forgotten about their "talk time." Sure enough, as soon as Daddy walked in the door, the two of them ran over to the chair. To this day, I'm not sure which one of them was more excited.

Days went by, and we saw a change in our son. His ability to sleep resumed. His anxiety dissipated. His joy returned. He also had a couple more brothers who were eager to get in line for some "talk time" with Daddy, but that's a story for another day.

The days of "talk time" have come and gone, but the value of them remains. We recently had the privilege of having our grown son home for the summer. "Talk time" unknowingly made its way back into our home. The discussions were no longer about Spiderman or Godzilla nor did our grown son sit on his dad's lap. However, they still included sharing from our hearts, praying for one another, laughing, and shedding tears. "Talk time" will forever be a highlight with each of our sons as we prioritize growing together and encouraging one another through these conversations.

As I think about our "talk times" with our sons, I am reminded of our "talk times" with our Heavenly Father. Even as adults, we have those nights when anxiety creeps its way into our bedrooms. The darkness overtakes us as stress invades our souls. The bedroom walls soon press in around us. Job dissatisfaction, financial challenges, or relationship struggles hang heavily in the air around us. We lie in our beds suffocated by the pressures that seem to steal the very breath within our lungs.

Thank goodness, the story doesn't end there, my friend. Here enters God. He's right there waiting to talk. He's ready to listen to you share your heart. He's ready to have you pray. He's ready to join you in laughter. He's ready to wipe the tears from your eyes as He comforts you during your struggles. As our Father, He highly anticipates time with His child because time with Him will bring about the change. I pray you set aside time today to climb up in His lap and pour your heart out to Him. Share with Him the struggles that are keeping you awake at night. Enjoy some "talk time" with the One who finds this time with you invaluable.

Ponder & Pray

Do you take time daily to spend time with your Heavenly Father? What will you commit to in order to ensure you don't miss out on the opportunity to allow Him to minister to you?

_____

_____

_____

_____

Heavenly Father, I thank you that you are a God who enjoys having your children spend time with you. I praise you for always being present and providing me with opportunities to "sit in the corner chair" with you. Would you please minister to me as I sit with you? Please bring me comfort today and equip me with all I need for the day ahead. Amen.

Day 10

Stick Attack

"Watch and pray so that you will not fall into temptation. The spirit is willing, but the flesh is weak."

Matthew 26:41

The day had finally arrived. My parents deemed my brother, sister, and I old enough to ride our bikes to our local swimming hole. Riding our bikes to the swimming hole was not in itself a new adventure. No, it was the fact that they were letting us make the trip on our own for the first time. Dressed in our suits, we hopped on our bikes and waved good-bye, knowing this was a landmark day. The day marked the first day of many where we gained greater independence to do things by ourselves because our parents trusted us.

Seated on our banana seat bikes, we raced to the end of our long driveway. We paused before hitting the country road. The two-mile ride ahead was filled with laughter and fun. My sister and I hugged the line on the side of the road while my brother passed by making "zooming" noises with no interest in hugging the sideline.

We eventually arrived at the beach, sweat trickling down our foreheads. Quickly dumping our bikes in the sand, all three of us ran toward the water with smiles as big as the horizon displayed before us. This was the life. We were grown up. We were enjoying the freedom offered to people mature enough to handle adventures without their parents.

The time in the water quickly passed by as we splashed and played tag. Before long, it was time for me, the oldest, to round everyone up to head for home.

"Hey guys! Time to hit the road!" I yelled as I made my way toward the shore.

My brother bolted past me, being sure to splash me as he passed. I joined him in running toward the shore as we raced one another to our bikes.

Suddenly, shrieks of fear pierced the air. We halted, and I am sure our hearts stopped beating for a moment. As we turned to look behind us, our younger sister screamed from the water, "Shark! Help! It's got me!" Her face was white, and terror filled her eyes.

We rushed towards our sister. She stood in knee deep water frantically flailing her arms and attempting to run. Her dilemma was that her legs weren't taking her anywhere. Oh, they were moving, almost as quickly as her mouth as she screamed again for us to save her from this "deadly shark attack." After assessing the situation, our hearts resumed beating. It was clear she was in no danger. My brother and I did what any good siblings would do - we laughed. And we laughed some more.

Not finding our lack of concern comforting, she continued to scream, "It's got me! Help me!" We momentarily wiped the smirks off our faces.

"Why don't you unhook your shirt from that stick you're caught on," my brother and I said simultaneously.

She paused her screaming for a moment to find she was indeed held captive by a stick. Sheepishly, she unhooked her shirt. We began laughing again about the "killer stick" that threatened the life of our sister.

It was definitely time for us to head home. My brother and I continued to laugh about the "shark" that lived in our freshwater bay. I don't recall my sister joining in on the laughter, but in her defense, we had recently watched the movie, *Jaws*.

There are plenty of times in our lives when we get caught by "sticks." Those times when we feel trapped, are unable to escape, and wish to scream for help. Sometimes, those sticks are because of a poor choice we made, and we are living with the consequences. Other times, those sticks are because others have made choices that are impacting our lives. Perhaps we are stuck in an addiction or buried under piles of debt. Maybe, we are living with the pain of an abusive relationship or trying to unhook ourselves from the pain of health issues.

These sticks make us feel out of control, often forcing us into a life of fear or depression. Yet, I want to remind you, we serve a God whose heart's desire is to rescue you and free you from those "sticks." Thankfully, He will react with compassion, love, and kindness, not the way my brother and I reacted. He will approach you in the midst of that fear and depression. Not only will He "unhook" you from that stick, He will take your hand and walk out of the water with you and never leave your side.

Ponder & Pray

Are there any sins or other circumstances in your life that cause you panic as you attempt to rescue yourself? Are you willing to give these to God today?

_____

_____

_____

_____

Lord, although I may laugh at the fact that this little girl mistook a stick for a shark, I acknowledge that I, too, have sin and situations in my life in which fear takes over my rational thought. Give me the strength to allow you to rescue me from those, replacing my panic with peace and my sin with salvation. Thank you for being my rescuer. Amen.

Day 11

Peter Pan

Jesus Christ is the same yesterday and today and forever.

Hebrews 13:8

The day had arrived. My son had reached a certain age, and my husband and I determined it was time to have "the talk" with him. The talk would include conversation about the changes his body was experiencing, would experience in the future, and the "s" word. Yes, I mean sex.

As a mom, I was a bit sad to be left out for this particular conversation, but I also felt excited. Excited about the special time my husband and son were going to have together as they discussed God's design for a man's body. I was sure it would be a memorable day for both of them. A day they would both look back on and cherish because it marked the beginning of our son's transition from a boy to a man. Yes, I am being a little sarcastic here. However, with this being our first son, I also did think this was going to be pretty cool for both of them.

I was gone that day to give them plenty of time for said conversation. Upon my return home, I decided to check with my son first. I was more than curious about how this discussion went and was looking forward to hearing his response or even if he had any questions he may want to ask his mom.

"So, you and Dad had a little talk today, huh?" I inconspicuously commented.

"Yup."

Hmmm. That was definitely not as much detail as I was hoping to hear. I decided to dig a little deeper.

"What did you think about the talk? Did you learn anything new? How did it go?" I pried.

My son quickly lifted his head and shot me a "you've got to be kidding me look" as he clearly and concisely said, "I can see why Peter Pan wanted to stay a boy."

Mic drop.

Whether we like it or not, change is inevitable. Our bodies change. Our jobs change. Our minds change. Seasons change. Thank goodness, even clothing styles change. It seems, that as one person put it, "the only thing permanent is change."

Yet, there is someone who, in the midst of all the constant changes around us, will never change. We serve a

God who is unchangeable. We serve a God who will stand firm and provide us with the unwavering platform to stand upon.

Hebrews 13:8 says, "Jesus is the same yesterday and today and forever." During my changes, I am thankful I have a Savior who will remain the same. Some changes I look forward to with great anticipation. Other changes slowly creep in and catch me off-guard. Still, others happen suddenly, leaving me flailing as I attempt to grasp something that will provide me stability and comfort.

I know you can relate. I know you have situations in your life that seem out of control. They may have crept their way in, creating anxiousness and uncertainty. Maybe they rushed in, swept you off your feet, and left pain and turmoil in their path.

Regardless of how they made their way into your life, please know you can rest in the One who does not change and will always be there to provide the comfort, safety, and stability you long to obtain. Rest in Him today. Allow Him to walk you through whatever changes have already made their way in as well as the ones that will make their way into your life in the future.

Are there any changes in your life that are creating anxiety or uncertainty? Will you release them to God today?

_____

_____

_____

_____

Dear Lord Jesus, there are some situations in my life in which I don't feel secure. I feel they are out of my control, and that creates anxiety. Please remove my insecurities and anxiousness. Fill me instead with your peace and a spirit of confidence as I rest in knowing you are in control. Amen.

Day 12

Childlike Prayer

Is anyone among you in trouble? Let them pray. Is anyone happy? Let
them sing songs of praise.

James 5:13

The smell of spaghetti wafted its way through the house. One of the little guys set down his toy trains and skipped into the kitchen to see if dinner was almost ready. He ran back to give his brothers the good news. "It's ready!" he yelled. The older boys jumped up from their seats in the living room and scrambled to find their chairs around the table. All five boys were eager to dive into one of their favorite family meals.

The typical dinnertime question came from Dad. "Who would like to pray today?" The older brothers smirked and looked at each other knowingly. Our then five-year-old raised his hand excitedly. "Me, Dad! I want to pray!"

"Dear Jesus, thank you for the day. I went to school today. I played trains. Glad we wrestled today. Cosmo jumped on me. I'm glad we read a book. I'm glad I'm gonna eat spaghetti. And thank you for the food. Amen."

As soon as "amen" was said, the brothers dug into their dinner but not without a couple more smiles between them and a pat on their little brother's shoulder. "Good job, buddy."

You see, Dad would ask this question daily. Without hesitation, this little guy would immediately raise his hand, nearly jumping out of his seat in excitement. When he prayed, he frequently went on and on and on, making way for some growling stomachs while we eagerly waited for "amen." However, it was a small sacrifice for how wonderful it was to hear his tiny voice talk to Jesus about every detail of his day.

The little guy who I'm referring to is now grown and attending college. Although I miss the joy of hearing the childlike prayer on a regular basis, I hold these memories close to my heart. What do you think it is about a child's prayer that melts the hearts of us adults? As I think back to those prayers, I wonder why adults don't often pray with the same enthusiasm and passion as a child. When do we lose some of that excitement to literally sit down with Jesus and tell Him about our day? As I look back on my son's prayer, I am reminded we can learn so much from watching our children pray.

For instance, I don't need eloquent speech when I talk to Jesus. He does not care if I pronounce words correctly or speak in proper sentences. I can share anything with Him, from the most trivial details of my day to the more complicated pieces. I bet He loved hearing from my five-year-old about his wrestling match and playing with the dog. Yet, somehow as adults, we guard our words more carefully. The temptation is almost to be calculated in our prayers as we cautiously choose what we say instead of just allowing God to hear all that is on our heart.

One of my favorite scriptures on prayer can be found in James 5:13. It says, "Is anyone of you in trouble? He should pray. Is anyone happy? Let him sing songs of praise." This verse takes me back to my son's prayers. At least once in every prayer, he would say the word "glad." That's exactly what the end of this verse is teaching us. God is saying, "Yes! Let me know when you are happy!" What a great challenge for us! If you're anything like me, it's easy to get caught up in laying the requests before the Lord. Sometimes, my list is quite extensive. Although this is certainly a portion of what the Lord desires from us during our prayer time, He also is clear about the delight He has when we share the "happy" parts of our lives too. Let us use my son's example today by adding gladness and praise to our prayer time. And may we do it with a child-like excitement.

How can you adapt the prayer below to take this opportunity to share with God some of the good things that have happened in your life recently?

_____

_____

_____

_____

Dear Jesus, thank you for this day. I got up and had fun visiting with my boys. I got to play some pickle-ball with them, which was really cool. I am glad I am healthy enough to enjoy a game with them. I'm glad my mom cooked a big meal for us before the boys had to head back to college and work. It was really good! Lastly, Lord, I'm glad I had time to reflect today. Through that reflection, you used the prayers of our little boy to remind me to pray with the heart of a child. Amen.

Day 13

Bridled Boredom

But seek first his kingdom and his righteousness, and all these things will be given to you as well.

Matthew 6:33

I hummed to the song playing on the radio, feeling quite accomplished by all I was getting done while my kids played quietly in their bedrooms. That was until I heard the pitter patter of small feet coming down the hallway.

I turned around to see one of my sons standing before me. He wore the dreaded "I'm bored" look all over his face. It's the look that puts even the best of moms over the edge. It's the look that brings shivers down our spines and causes our eyes to roll deep into the back of our heads. Here it was, staring straight at me.

I can handle this, I thought. He doesn't even have the words out of his mouth yet, so I know I have time to prepare my script for him. As if on cue, the words poured out of his mouth, "Mom, I'm bored." With all my might, I attempted to contain the shivers and hold the eye roll. I began to share with him the great wisdom I had to impart. I began with the whole "boredom is just a state of mind… that perhaps he just needed to get creative…to have a better attitude." As he turned to leave the room, I had this sinking feeling that my great wisdom hit flat. If I'm not mistaken, it was his eyes that were rolling.

Nonetheless, he was out of the kitchen, and I was able to continue with my work. For two minutes anyway. Then, he marched right back into the kitchen. "Mom, I'm still bored." This time, I was able to remind him of the giant toybox that was overflowing in his room. If he couldn't find something to play with, we could just give those toys away. Although this method had done nothing for me as a child, I thought maybe it would work on my child. Instead, I was met with another eye roll and a spirit of disappointment.

I plowed forward with my work, ignoring his disappointment. He slumped and shuffled his way out of the kitchen only to return. "Now, I just told you…". He interrupted me midsentence, looked me in the eyes, and said, "Mom, I don't want to play toys. I just want to play with you."

My heart suddenly softened. I realized my cleaning could wait; my son needed some attention right now.

Can you relate to this, my friend? All too often, the loud cry of the "to do" list overshadows the more important cries within our homes. Unfortunately, the list stops us not only from engaging with our family, but it also diverts our attention from time with our Heavenly Father. As we continue to be laser-focused on our list, it's almost as if we are saying, "Just go to the other room, Lord. I have some great things I'm accomplishing today; I'm on a roll. I'm sure we can have some time together later in the day." I can picture God putting His head down in disappointment as He shares, "Misty, I don't want you accomplishing those things right now. I just want time with you."

As you go about your day, determine to set the lists aside to enjoy time focusing on the people around you and the God who is waiting to sit with you for a bit. Please remember, the lists will always be there; the jobs will always need to be completed. However, the time to build a closer relationship with those around you and with Him is today. In fact, it is right now.

Ponder & Pray

Have you pushed important people and/or God away from you as you fill your time with less important activities?

_____

_____

_____

_____

Lord, please forgive me for putting my seemingly endless to-do list in front of my relationship with others and with you. Please use your gentle voice of conviction to pull me close to you, reminding me to keep my priorities in line with your desires for my life. Amen.

Day 14

Security Reigns

I keep my eyes always on the Lord. With him at my right hand,
I will not be shaken.

Psalm 16:8

The day at my grandparent's house was once again filled with fun and laughter. My siblings and I rolled down the big hill in their yard, stopping just before landing in the river at the bottom. We hid in the pine forest across the street, and then returned to their home for some treats that Grandma had waiting for us.

All too quickly, our time together came to a close. We shared hugs and said our good-byes. We watched as Grandma and Grandpa ran across their tiny home to the bedroom window, just in time to see us wave good-bye as we pulled out of the driveway.

After a stimulating day like that, it wasn't surprising when my brother, sisters, and I all succumbed to sleep. My plan was to "pretend sleep" in case my parents decided to converse about anything interesting. However, I was no match for the comfortable weight of my sister's head upon my shoulder and the whirring of the tires. The car fell into a peaceful silence. Sleep quickly overtook me, but not before I heard my mom whisper to my dad, "Yup, looks like they're all asleep already."

A sense of security still washes over me when I think back on those childhood drives. I rested in the backseat completely unaware of any dangers my parents may have avoided along the road. I'm sure there were times when deer darted onto the roadway or when my dad had to make his way through weather that created challenges along the way. And yet, there wasn't a concern in my mind. With my head leaned against the window, I rested with complete assurance that I was safe and secure. My two protectors were in the front seat, and I knew without a doubt, my parents would lovingly deliver me to my destination.

Life often mirrors those drives. While some roads are safe and easy to navigate, other roads are a bit scarier. There are roads that contain illness, relationship pain, or fear of the unknown. At other points, we travel down the road without issue only to be jarred awake by a pothole. This pothole threatens to swallow us, stealing security from us in an instant. We realize that security doesn't seem as simple as it did in those childhood days.

I imagine you can relate to the developing challenges we come across on our daily travels. It can be difficult to travel even a day without concern or worry creeping in, attempting to bring anxiety, depression, and fear into our path.

Yet, God gives us promises, such as this verse in Psalm 4 that says, "I will lie down and sleep in peace, for you alone, O Lord, make me dwell in safety." We can be secure in knowing that regardless of what road we may travel, we have someone in the driver's seat who is prepared to make the journey with us. Although He does not promise there won't be obstacles along the way, He does promise us He will provide us with peace and security. He will not only provide us with security on this earth, but upon trusting in Him, He provides us eternal security.

I pray today you are able to rest securely in the truth that Jesus loves you and He will walk this journey of life with you. He will deliver you to your destination, and He won't take His eyes off you. If you aren't secure in knowing your eternal destination, I pray you do that today by letting Him know you desire a relationship with Him.

In what areas of your life are you feeling insecure about your journey? Are you allowing God to provide you the peace and security you need?

_____

_____

_____

_____

Heavenly Father, I desire to be secure in knowing you are walking with me on this earthly journey as well as in my eternal journey. I choose to trust you in every way. I thank you for never leaving my side on this journey we call life. I often get tired, insecure, and even fearful of what may lie around the next bend. Please remind me in a very tangible way today that you are present with me. Allow me to sense your loving arms around me as you remove the feelings that are not of you and replace them with all of the glorious blessings you have in store for me. Thank you, Lord Jesus. Amen.

Day 15

Matchbox Giveaway

And do not forget to do good and to share with others, for with such sacrifices God is pleased.

Hebrews 13:16

With five boys in the house, we had no shortage of Matchbox ® cars. Because of the fifteen-year age spread between the youngest and the oldest, some of our cars were tattered, reflecting their age, while others were bright and shiny, having been added more recently. No matter how many times I allowed the younger boys to pick a toy from the grocery store, they always headed to the Matchbox ® section. I was continually amazed that they never chose one they already had at home. It would seem a limit could be reached on how many a family could have before duplicates were collected; but if this were the case, our family never experienced it.

What I did know was that these cars were special to them. They would line them up from one end of the living room to the other according to style, color, and any other ways they could imagine. They would spend hours creating their own little "car world." Knowing how special these cars were to them, I was completely caught off guard one cold December day.

Our church announced they were doing a mission outreach, which included collecting and sending Matchbox ® cars to children in Haiti for Christmas. The cars could be gently used. Not really expecting a response, my husband delivered this announcement to our boys. He asked them if they would like to donate any of their cars to the children in Haiti.

To our surprise, the boys grabbed a plastic bag and ran down the hallway to their bedroom. The clanking of toys and enthusiastic voices could be heard from the kitchen. Soon, they stood before us with a bag of their cars all set to donate to the children in Haiti.

The boys excitedly set the bag by the door, so it was ready to take with them to church that night. They eagerly anticipated making the delivery.

Upon our arrival at the church, I led the boys to the lady in charge of outreach and told them they could give their bag of cars to her. Disappointed, they slowly handed over their bag. It wasn't until later we realized our boys thought they were personally going to deliver the toys to the children in Haiti. Apparently, we didn't explain the logistics of this outreach very well.

While tucking my then seven-year-old in bed that night, he asked what I thought the children in Haiti might do with the cars when they received them. Laughing, he said, "Maybe, they will smash them into each other like we do!" I joined him in the laughter and said, "Yes, I think they will do exactly that."

After a quick pause and one final kiss good-night, I headed toward the bedroom door. However, I wasn't quite out of the room yet when he surprised me once again.

"Mom, when we give stuff to people who don't have as much as we do, I get tears in my eyes like I have right now. It actually makes me have this good feeling inside my body."

I guess I hadn't given him the final kiss good-night. I headed back to his bed, wrapped him in my arms, and thanked God for another lesson spoken through the heart of a child. And yes, we both had tears in our eyes.

Isn't it a wonderful thing when our eyes are opened through the wisdom of a child? I love how God is able to speak to us through our children. I wonder, when was the last time we gave something to someone that caused us to get tears in our eyes or have a "good feeling inside our body?" It's generally when our giving has been sacrificial. When we have truly given something that was a treasure to us, something valuable to us personally. Something, perhaps, like a toy is to a child.

Our world is filled with people who are in need right now. I pray we will allow God to open our eyes to truly see the needs around us. I pray He will fill our hearts with compassion and allow us to experience what it means to give sacrificially. God's desire is to use us to meet the needs of others, to help them during their difficulties, to encourage them when they are struggling, and to lend a hand when they are weary.

Will you pause today and ask God who He would have you help? It might be a neighbor who needs a visit; a family who needs some groceries; a couple who needs a night out; a single parent who needs childcare; or a child who needs shoes. The needs are great, but so are the list of opportunities to help.

What Matchbox® gift will you offer to someone? I guarantee when it is led by God and given from the heart, you, too, will be able to experience a tear and a "good feeling inside your body."

What will you do today to help someone in need?

_____

_____

_____

_____

Heavenly Father, I come to you today to thank you for all you have blessed me with, which is much more than I ever deserve. I know there are many who aren't as fortunate as me, so I ask you today to specifically direct me to someone I can bless. Show me the person. Show me the need. Convict my heart to follow through on your lead today. Amen.

Day 16

Freedom to Ride

When I am afraid, I put my trust in you.

Psalm 56:3

My youngest son enthusiastically entered the house. He quickly explained to me that his friend, who was "two whole years younger" than him, knew how to ride a "two-wheeled bike."

"He doesn't even have training wheels anymore, Mom."

I let him know that maybe this was the summer he could ride a two-wheeler too.

My mind flashed back to last summer when my husband went out to the shed and removed the training wheels off our son's bike. Cheering as he ran behind the bike, my husband let go and allowed our son to ride on his own.

However, after a couple spills and scrapes, our son decided the two-wheeler just wasn't for him. He wanted to have the stability, safety, and control that the extra little wheels gave him. It definitely was less painful to continue to drive around with training wheels.

But this year, this year would be different, our son assured me as he waited for his daddy to arrive home from work. After giving Daddy a few minutes to grab a coffee, he rushed him out the door. The bike was set out and all ready for the training wheels to be removed.

Within minutes, the training wheels were off, and our son was on the seat of the bike. I quickly ran in the house to grab my camera, wanting to capture this epic event. By the time I returned outside, I could hear our son yelling, "Watch Mom! No training wheels!"

There he was, zipping across the yard as if he had been doing it all his life. His fear of falling had suddenly been replaced by the feeling of freedom. My husband and I smiled as we took one another's hand. Our youngest son was now riding a two-wheeler.

Jolting us from our moment of reflection was a loud, yet distant voice. The breeze was carrying our son's voice across our large yard and planting it deeply within our ears. At first, I thought maybe he was injured; however, that wasn't the tone at all. Neither was it a "mom, watch this" type of voice. Instead, it was a joy-filled, "this is awesome" shout coming from a little boy as he rounded a corner at top speed. The words faded into the background as his bright eyes and beaming smile perfectly spoke what was needed in the moment.

As I think back upon that day, it causes me to wonder if we go through our lives with training wheels. Instead of experiencing the freedom of life without the training wheels, we choose the stability, safety, and control of keeping those wheels tightly secured. We desire a life with no spills, no scrapes. A life with the least amount of pain as possible. A life that is impossible to have on this side of heaven.

Yet, we serve a God, our Heavenly Father, who desires to remove the training wheels. Our Father wants to show us how to trust Him and how to give Him control. He wants us to know that when there is a spill or scrapes, He will be right there to pick us up, reassure us, and put us back on the bike.

Perhaps you are like me, and you find it difficult to allow Him to remove those training wheels. In our minds, we know we can trust Him, yet our hearts continue to want control. We fight for control over the relationships in our lives. We attempt to control every detail of the finances. We struggle to trust Him with the health of our families. Does this sound familiar? Eventually, we give up control only to backslide and throw those training wheels back on again and again as uncertainties arise.

Can you commit to stopping the cycle? I pray you are able to place your trust in your Heavenly Father today. He desires to see you riding in freedom, rounding the corner at top speed, and fully trusting in Him as you let out a joy-filled "this is awesome!"

Ponder & Pray

What area of your life do you find challenging to turn over to God? Are you willing to give that to Him today?

_____

_____

_____

_____

Heavenly Father, I struggle to let go of control. I hold tightly to my struggling finances, relationships, and health. In my mind, I know giving it to you is the better way; yet, in my heart, I still hold on, fearful of releasing it. Fearful of the unknown. Fearful of losing control. I ask that you would remove that fear from my heart and replace it with faith. The type of faith that understands you are much more able to carry these issues than I. Please give me the strength and the boldness to remove the training wheels and ride my two-wheeler in the freedom you provide. Amen.

Day 17

Hiding in Plain Sight

Nothing in all creation is hidden from God's sight. Everything is
uncovered and laid bare before the eyes of him to whom

we must give account.

Hebrews 4:13

My vivacious sister, who is ten years younger than me, was ready to play one of her favorite games, hide-and-seek. As a three-year-old, her energy was unmatched by anyone else in the home as were her choices of hiding places.

I closed my eyes to count. I could hear her behind me whispering to my siblings, "Put me in the clothes hamper." This was her hiding place of choice recently, and she rarely departed from it.

"Are you ready?" I asked.

"Yes!" I could hear her giggle and instruct our other siblings to keep her secret by putting her chubby, little fingers to her mouth to shush them.

Standing up, I glanced around the room, avoiding eye contact with the little girl whose head stuck out from the top of the hamper. With hair standing on end because of the static electricity, her smile was as large as the pile of clothes that had been displaced.

"I wonder where she could be? Mandy! Where are you?" I chanted over and over.

I made my way around the room, checking in spaces that would have been impossible for her to fit, like behind the desk. "No, not there."

"Maybe, she's under the table," I said, crawling on the floor under the table. "Nope. She's not under here either. Hmmm. Where could she be?"

As I searched through the laundry pile next to the hamper, I could feel her eyes looking down on me. "No, not in this clothes pile. Huh, I wonder what this pile of clothes is doing on the floor?"

By this time, the giggling could not be contained. "I better put these clothes back into the hamper where they belong," I explained, struggling to withhold my own giggles. As I threw laundry on her head, she could not restrain her excitement any longer. "I'm right here!" she shouted. Her hands reached up to me as she waited for me to pull her out of the hamper.

I imagine we all wish we could go back to the old days of hide and seek. Oh, I don't mean we run to the clothes hamper and hide beneath the pile of clothes, although sometimes that may seem tempting. I do mean we continue to have those times when we desire to hide not only from our problems and our family but also from our God.

When we think of my sister in the hamper, "hiding in plain sight," we chuckle at our own memories of playing this game. We recognize she wasn't hidden at all. We understand she was in the sightline of the seeker (me) the entire time. And yet, it's easy to find ourselves playing the same game in our lives. We do our best to hide from people who have hurt us or make us feel uncomfortable. We hide our fears of failure or an unknown future. Sometimes, we hide our dreams because they seem beyond reach. We are afraid certain people will think that there is no way we could accomplish that goal. Perhaps we hide our loneliness. We cover it with our smiles, our joking, and our "I'm fine" attitudes.

People are not the only ones from whom we hide. We tend to save our best hiding places for God. Hiding from our Heavenly Father is not only impossible, but it isn't helpful. Thankfully, God continues to seek after us, regardless of where we are hiding. He waits for us to say to Him, "I'm right here!" He longs to pull us from the hamper, look into our eyes, and let us know that He sees our fears, dreams, and loneliness. Most importantly, He lets us know we are unable to find a place to hide where He will not continue to seek us and ultimately, find us.

I hope you will rest in knowing God sees you right where you are today. He sees you right there in the midst of whatever your situation. He desires to be in the midst of your fears. He desires to awaken your forgotten dreams.

He longs to meet you in your loneliness. Be real with Him today. Come out from your "hiding" and enjoy spending some time sharing with Him how you are feeling.

Ponder & Pray

What feelings, fears, or dreams are you
hiding from God today?

_____

_____

_____

_____

Dear Lord, I don't even understand why I attempt to hide from you. My brain knows I am unable to do so, yet so many emotions convince me that I should. Sometimes, it's fear. Sometimes, it's loneliness. Sometimes, it's the feeling that I'm not enough. Other times, I'm just too exhausted to function, so I try to disappear. Thank you for reminding me today that not only am I unable to hide from you, but that you don't want me hiding from you. Thank you for reminding me you desire to spend time with me. Thank you for reminding me you see me, regardless of what emotions I am carrying. Thank you for seeing me in my hiding place. Amen.

Day 18

Alphabet Cereal

Heal me, Lord, and I will be healed; save me and I will be saved,
for you are the one I praise.

Jeremiah 17:14

It was one of those mornings that are hard to come by as a mom. You know the ones I am talking about - a peaceful one. Our two oldest boys had left for school. The three youngest boys had just finished their breakfast and were off to the living room to play. *Ah, yes*, I thought, sitting down at the table with my tea. *I have a couple minutes of peace.*

As a mom for eighteen years at that point, I should have known that silence when dealing with three children under the age of six does not usually mean peace. Nevertheless, it was so nice. I just wanted to savor it, even if only for a couple sips of tea. As I rationalized that the couple minutes

85

of peace would certainly outweigh whatever it was that was creating the silence, the three little guys ran into the room jarring me from my thoughts.

"Mom! Mom! Look what we did!" they simultaneously yelled as they ran into the room excited and filled with a sense of accomplishment. "We dumped the WHOLE box of cereal on the floor!"

Really? This was something to be excited about? This was something to celebrate? This was something to come proudly before your mom to share with her? Oh my. In that moment, I had a decision to make. I needed to make it quickly.

As I walked into the living room to see the entire box of cereal scattered on the carpet, two options sped through my mind. I could loudly speak the words that were on my mind at that particular moment. "What in the world were you thinking? What a mess!" Or, I could go with the option only a minute part of me wanted to choose. I took a deep breath and said, "Look, it's alphabet cereal! Let's work together to see how many letters and words we can find as we pick it up."

And so, the game began. I named a letter. They scurried around the floor grabbing all those letters and putting them into the bowl. I spelled a word, and they sifted through the letters looking for the correct ones to create the word. We soon had a clean floor, happy children, and a mom who would probably handle the silence a little differently next time.

As I consider those pieces of cereal strewn across the floor, I think about how my Heavenly Father sees the pieces of my life on some days. Oh, what a mess I can make sometimes from poor decisions in spending to impatience with my children to speaking down to my spouse. All of these pieces can create the image of a life in shambles.

Do you ever feel like your life is a big mess spread across the floor? I think there are even times when our messes appear so big, it seems clean-up is far from possible. In those moments, I feel God wants to say to us, "What in the world were you thinking? What a mess!" Yet, He speaks to us gently and acknowledges the mess. With Him, we can pick up the pieces, one at a time, and clean up the mess we created. He can direct us in our finances. He can prompt us to be patient with our children when we feel out of control. He can fill our hearts and minds with positive words to speak to our spouse. When we ask Him for direction and allow Him to lead the process, He can teach us every step of the way.

Today, I encourage you to ask God for forgiveness for those days you have made a mess out of your life. Remember, He is a God who forgives. He is also a God of new beginnings and a God who loves you through your mistakes. Regardless of the mess, it is never too big for Him. He desires to walk with you through whatever your clean-up may look like, all the while putting the pieces of your life back together. Also remember that those around you will continue to create messes. Some will be messes around the house, like my little guys created, but others could be messes created from poor life decisions. During that time, it is our challenge to react in the same manner of love and forgiveness that our Heavenly Father has so graciously offered to us.

Ponder & Pray

What decisions have you made that you think have made a "mess" out of part of yours or someone else's life? Have you spoken to God about those messes and asked for His guidance in the clean-up process?

_____

_____

_____

_____

Heavenly Father, I thank you that through normal daily activities, you are able to teach me about patience, love, and forgiveness. I ask that you would forgive me for the messes I have created in the lives of others and in my own life. I praise you for loving me enough to walk beside me while we put the pieces of my life back together. I also ask you, Lord, that you would direct my thoughts and actions, so I am open to reacting to others in a way that mimics you and brings you glory, honor, and praise. Amen.

Day 19

Stuck in the Mud

Pride brings a person low, but the lowly in spirit gain honor.

Proverbs 29:23

Growing up on a farm provided many opportunities for great adventures. Springtime was especially ripe with excitement. As the robins began to sing, our little grove of trees in the backyard looked more enticing. Perhaps it was time to start building our forts in it again. As the snow in our long driveway melted away, it made way for a race-track. It was time to haul the bikes out of the shed. The field around our home thawed, creating acres of marvel-ous…mud. Yes, mud.

For me, the mud actually didn't appear too marvelous. However, to my younger brother and sister, it was exactly that, "marvelous mud." Where I simply saw disgusting dirt, they saw the opportunity to have some fun on the farm. An opportunity to do something that could only be done in the spring when the ground was thawing. An opportunity to go exploring in the field.

One spring morning on his way out to the shed, my dad gave the three of us specific instructions not to go into the field. He went on to state that the thaw was happening at such a quick speed the mud would suck our little boots right into the ground.

Content with my dad's instructions, my siblings and I began to play outside. We rode bikes and continued creating our forts. Soon, the bike riding and fort building were not enough for my sister and brother; they just couldn't take it. It was like the mud in the field was calling out their names.

"Come play with me," the field echoed.

"Just one step in the field won't hurt anything," it continued, tempting them.

Listening to their discussion with my big sister ears, I reminded them, "Dad said we can't go out there today you guys!"

With their younger sibling nonverbals, they quickly brushed away this bossy, boring sister and ran toward the field. Their boots barely stayed on their feet as they laughed and raced to where the grass met the mud. That's where they stopped.

Intrigued by them, I followed, wondering if they would do it. Would they take that step - the step Dad specifically told them not to take - into the field?

Looking at each other one last time, they charged for the mud with a nod of their heads and smile on their faces. One step. Safe. This isn't bad. Two steps in. Yes, we're doing well. It's not as sticky as Dad said it was. Three steps in proved a little more challenging as they attempted to lift their feet for step four. However, by step four, they were stuck. There would be no step five. They looked at each other before turning to me and yelling, "We're stuck! Help! We're stuck!"

Being the big sister, I knew I needed to be the one who would go for help. My heart began to pound as I thought about delivering this message to my dad.

Running out to the barn, I yelled, "They're stuck, Dad. They went in the field and got stuck!" Dad didn't need any more information. He set aside his task to rush to my siblings' aid. My mind flashed with pride as I thought, "But not me, Dad. I listened and didn't go into the field, just like you said."

I was sent into the house as my dad made his way to rescue the stuck siblings. I parked myself at the window to get the best view. I remember peering out the window and watching Dad begin the process of pulling them free. Patting myself on the back for my obedience, I enjoyed watching the rescue unfold.

My dad made his way into the field. His more than six-foot frame towered over them as he grabbed hold of each sibling and pulled. He pulled some more. With a couple more pulls and a couple less boots on their feet, they were finally free. He set them on solid ground, said a few words, and walked away. To this day, I am pretty sure there are a couple boots still in that field. These boots remain forever lost to the depths of the earth because the temptation of mud just simply looked too fun to ignore.

As I wrote this, my thought was to create today's devotion based on temptation and how God rescues us from it. I could use the "marvelous mud" to create an analogy. The mud called to them and tempted them to do exactly what their dad had asked them not to do. When they disobeyed, their dad came and rescued them from the very thing he had asked them not to mess with in the first place. The analogy seemed so clear to me that it almost, yes, almost covers up another sin that was taking place at the same time. Did you catch it?

Pride. Oh, how sneaky our pride can be. Big Sister me was just full of it. From the beginning, I felt prideful because I wouldn't make the decision to disobey my dad. I felt prideful when my siblings were going to succumb to the temptation because I knew that I would make the decision to back away from it. I had plenty of pride to go around as I almost excitedly delivered the news to our dad that they had done what he had asked them to avoid. My prideful enjoyment hit its peak as I watched with a smirk in my heart my siblings get pulled from their sin.

Pride can so easily seep its way into our hearts. I can remember times I watched someone fall from a position of authority. I shook my head and inwardly boasted, "I would never do that!" Other moments, I privately proclaimed, "My children would never make that decision." I have been a part of projects where I allowed pride to enter because I was sure I could have accomplished the project far better. Still other times, I sat on my "high horse" and secretly celebrated the consequences someone "deserved" because he or she made a bad choice. Can you relate to any of those feelings? I am sure I am not alone.

Let us not be deceived, my friend. Pride is a sneaky and horribly destructive sin. It enters us in a small dose but grows into an ugly beast when it remains unchecked. Sometimes, it is so destructive, so ugly, and so deceiving that it convinces us that it doesn't exist.

Let us beware today of the sneaky sin of pride. Let us prayerfully examine our hearts, allowing God to point out the places where pride may be hiding. Then, let us ask Him for forgiveness, as we move ahead with a newfound freedom of being pulled out of the sin by the Dad who loves us so very much.

Ponder & Pray

When was the last time you were caught in the sin of pride? Did you ask God to free you from it?

_____

_____

_____

_____

Heavenly Father, I acknowledge that the temptations in my world today are innumerable. They seem to be reaching for me around every corner. Yet, as I ask you for strength to resist those temptations, I also ask you to remove the sin of pride that has already made a home in my heart. Forgive me for the comparisons I make with others and for the times I cut others down in my mind while I elevate myself. Thank you for the love and grace you provide as you rescue me from the mud-like temptations as well as the sins that I am already harboring. Amen.

Day 20

Clear Vision

Because of the Lord's great love, we are not consumed, for his compassions never fail. They are new every morning; great is your faithfulness.

Lamentations 3:22-23

The complaining from my son was beginning to take a toll on me as I drove him to town to pick up his new glasses.

"But I don't want to wear glasses, Mom," he whined as we walked into the office.

Before long, he was seated for the fitting, which was uneventful and completed quickly. He then irritably marched out of the office and back to the car with glasses in hand (unfortunately, not on his face).

As I started the car, I looked in my rearview mirror and

instructed him to try the glasses on for a few minutes. After flashing me the "I can't believe your making me do this" look, he groaned loudly and placed the glasses on his face. Satisfied, I began to back out of the parking spot.

Suddenly, I heard excitement my son's voice. "Mom! Look! There are birds on the telephone wire!"

I smiled and nodded as I listened to him continue. "Hey, I can read the sign that's way up the road, Mom! And look at the shapes of the clouds right there!"

As we traveled home, he continued to share with me the wonderful things that his "new eyes" were allowing him to see.

Although many years have passed since my son received his "new eyes," I can still hear the excitement in his voice. The awe and wonder as he told me about the birds on the wire. The amazement in being able to read the signs. The joy of seeing shapes in the clouds. His excitement was so evident; it encouraged me to pause and look around the world that day with fresh eyes of my own.

My son's reaction to experiencing the world through "new eyes" that day had me reflect on people seeing God for the first time. Have you met someone who has a newfound joy in the Lord? Sometimes, the joy is shining from someone who began a new relationship with Jesus or experienced God in a fresh way. Other times, this joy comes from a person who recently learned something new about God. When their eyes are opened, there may be singing. They may jump for joy or shout praises. Others are more restrained. You may see their joy through the tears trickling down their cheeks. Regardless of the expression, the excitement is contagious. It draws us in and we soon find ourselves experiencing it with them.

Have you allowed your joy in the Lord to fade? It's easy to allow the excitement of our relationship with Jesus to take a backseat to problems that arise. It's tempting to take new experiences with Him for granted. Yet, when this often-unintentional pattern settles into our spirits, the singing stops. The jumping settles. The tears subside. Those around us no longer sense our excitement.

Today, I hope you are able to take a step back from the worries of the day and see God as if for the first time. I hope you will allow Him to renew your eyes, so you can truly see His goodness. Take a journey back in time and revisit what it was like when you first experienced God. Life often beats us down to the point we forget to acknowledge the wonder all around us. Can you put your "new glasses" on your face today and once again experience the awe, the amazement, and the joy that your Savior has to offer you?

Ponder & Pray

What will you look at it today with fresh eyes? Will you allow God to show you the goodness surrounding you?

_____

_____

_____

_____

Dear Lord, I ask that you would give me "new eyes" today. Remind me again what it is like to see you for the first time. My heart's desire is to experience the awe, wonder, amazement, and joy all over again. May those things be new to me every morning as I seek to never take you for granted. Amen.

Day 21

Scattered Pieces

"For I know the plans I have for you," declares the Lord. "Plans to
prosper you and not to harm you, plans to give you hope and a future."
Jeremiah 29:11

I called them our "crazy days." It was the time in our life when we had a fifteen-, ten-, and four-year-old as well as our "babies," twenty months and newborn. Many days, it was all I could do to just get out of bed and make it through all the "normal" activities, like getting kids off to school, attending ballgames, and preparing meals. The laundry would pile up until I couldn't see the floor (or the wash machine for that matter). Often, the dishes would cover the countertop and fill the sink. We tripped over toys as we made our way over to the couch. Oh, those were the days.

Everyone's "crazy days" look different. They may pop up at a variety of stages in our lives. They are the times we wonder if we are appreciated or if we have any personal value at all. I have been there. The thoughts of my worthiness would come into question as I sat on my couch in the same milk-soaked t-shirt I wore the day prior. I wondered if anyone appreciated the number of diapers I changed and meals I cooked. During another stage of life, those thoughts came when my husband and I were working many hours. Our schedules were not matching up well. Time with him was limited, and I began to feel anxious. Was married life really supposed to look like this? If you have those feelings, you are certainly not alone. Yet, the lie within says we are the only ones walking through this season. Surely no one else has such thoughts. We become secluded or, in the least, bury those feelings for fear of being found out by someone. Those are such lies. Please don't believe them.

I talk to many young moms who are in the middle of those "crazy days." They wonder how they are going to have the energy to make it through or when they will be able to see beyond the diapers and dishes. Although many don't want to admit it for fear of being judged, the thoughts of *is this all there is* and *when do I get a life* come popping into their minds. Have you been there?

Maybe your "crazy days" have been the times when you were stuck in a job you didn't enjoy. Perhaps they came at a time when you were out of a job and the search for work felt hopeless. The stress continues to build, and you may feel as if you can't find your way out of the pit in which you have fallen. Have you been there?

Perhaps you are living your "crazy days" within your marriage. You don't see how it's going to survive; the pain seems unbearable. Maybe it's your finances; you don't see any hope for improvement. Your "crazy days" could be a time in your life when you felt alone. When life lacked purpose, and you were struggling to find your way. The list of possibilities is endless. The fact is we all have experienced these feelings at some point in our life.

Imagine our life is a puzzle. Our circumstances and life situations are represented by the pieces of said puzzle. It's not a completed puzzle but a puzzle which is scattered across a tabletop. Some of the pieces may have fallen on the floor while others are flipped upside down. Other pieces may appear to be missing; maybe they are lost under the couch. There are some pieces we view and question whether they even go in the same box as the others. Perhaps there are pieces we want to remove because we don't want them to be a part of our puzzle; we want to throw those pieces in the trash. Other pieces don't seem to fit at all for the puzzle. They are the wrong color, size, or material. When we try to make sense of them, they seem awkward; we can't even wedge them between pieces. We don't see a use for them, let alone find any value in them.

Thank goodness, it is not for us to make sense of the puzzle! I am reminded of Jeremiah 29:11, which says, "For I know the plans I have for you, declares the Lord. Plans to prosper you and not to harm you, plans to give you hope and a future." This verse cuts through the lies; it gives hope. This verse is in no way written in a light, fluffy way. It was written when the people of Israel were going through a very challenging time, a time when they felt hopeless. That is what makes it so powerful. It serves as a reminder that regardless of how messy those puzzle pieces appear, there is Someone who knows how to put the puzzle together. We serve a God who can take the pieces that look out of place and fit them. He is able to find that missing piece from under the couch, pick it up, wipe it off, and put it right where it belongs.

You can rejoice today in knowing God sees your finished product. The finished product is created through all of your upside down, strangely shaped, and even, lost pieces. That finished product may take a while to build and will even be painful at times; but when it is finished, that finished product is beautiful. That finished product is you.

What part of your life feels like it is scattered across a tabletop, needing God to put it back together?

_____

_____

_____

_____

Dear Lord, I come to you today to lay the scattered pieces of my life at your feet. Although my life appears to be a mess, I can trust you to pick up the pieces and put them together in a way that glorifies you. Thank you for connecting with me during the challenging times, mending my heart during the painful times, and seeing the big picture for my life. Amen.

Tuck-n-Run

*Jesus answered, "It is written: 'Man shall not live on bread alone, but
on every word that comes from the mouth of God'."*

Matthew 4:4

"Hurry up, guys! It doesn't take that long to brush your teeth."

"What do you mean you need another glass of water? I just gave you one."

"You need to go potty…again?"

It was no small task rounding up our five sons for bed. The words, "it's time for bed," would barely leave my mouth before the boys would rattle off an impressive list of questions or ideas that needed immediate attention. My husband and I felt quite accomplished when we were finally able get them contained in the living room for our family prayer time. The task was far from complete, however. We still needed to get them tucked into bed. Though exhausted from the day, we would make our way around to each of their beds, give them a kiss and hug, and wish them a good night's sleep. During one such bedtime, our then nine-year-old son presented a question that caught us off guard.

As my husband and I prepared to shut off the lights of the bedroom, a little voice spoke from the corner of the room.

"Dad, why do you always do the tuck-n-run?"

My husband and I looked at each other confused, but also curious. "What's the tuck-n-run?" my husband asked.

"Well Dad, it's when you come in here and give me my kiss and hug, say good night, and then leave the room really fast. You tuck-n-run."

That was all the conviction my husband needed that night. He walked back into the bedroom and laid on the bed with our son. They enjoyed some conversation before the lights went out that night. I believe the conversation had something to do with Dad explaining how blood gets to the end of a finger. We all know that the time together had less to do with the topic of the conversation and more to do with the fact that the tuck-n-run had no place in the room that evening.

As I consider the words of my son, I wonder how often I pull the tuck-n-run on my Heavenly Father. I wake up in the morning fully intending to spend time with Him.

However, before I know it, my mind is moving a million different directions. I make my way to my to-do list for the day without a second thought to spending time with my Savior. There are other times I plan to finish the day by thanking God for His blessings and reading some scripture. Instead, I find myself pulling the tuck-n-run as I hop in bed, reach for my phone, or turn on a mindless movie before falling to sleep. I leave God, who has eagerly been awaiting our time together, with the scraps of my day. He is left without the connection He desires because I didn't make Him a priority.

Remember that little voice in the corner of the room, my son's voice? Let us imagine that the voice is our Savior's. He clearly tells us in His Word that spending time with Him needs to be a priority. He continually reminds us that His Word and His voice are intended to feed us and give us nourishment throughout the day.

If you struggling to make time with Jesus a priority, I would like to offer a couple tips. I have not generally been a morning person. However, when I get up a little early and set time aside for Him at the beginning of the day, it sets a much better course for my day. I find that if I wait to spend time with Jesus till some later point, the day tends to come and go without the opportunity to spend time with Him. If you have little ones at home, have your Bible and devotion book handy. Place it near a spot you find yourself in often throughout the day, such as sitting right next to your favorite chair. When my children were young, I remember sitting in my chair rocking one of them while another played and using that time slot as my Jesus-time.

I hope today you take the time to pause and plan when your next Jesus-time will take place. Make avoiding the "tuck-n-run" temptation your first step towards accomplishing your Jesus-time plan.

Ponder & Pray

What will you do to commit to making the relationships with your loved ones and God a priority today?

_____

_____

_____

_____

Heavenly Father, forgive me for the times when I put my schedule, job, and other activities in front of you and my loved ones. Please speak to my heart to remind me to slow down and enjoy time with my loved ones and with you. I look forward to sharing with you the special times with my family. I also desire to share with you the simplest details of my days, my heart of gratitude, and my struggles. I commit today to do away with the tuck-n-run and instead, run into your arms where I am fed by your very presence. Amen.

Day 23

❀

Teamwork Works

And let us consider how we may spur one another on toward love and
good deeds, not giving up meeting together, as some are in the habit of
doing, but encouraging one another and all the more
as you see the Day approaching.

Hebrews 10:24-25

"When can we go, Mom? Aren't you ready yet?"
These questions frequently came out of my children's mouths during the summer months as they eagerly anticipated visits to Grandma and Grandpa's house to swim and play at the pond.

Packing up suits, towels, snacks, and toys, we were ready to spend the day by the water. Before the car completely stopped, the boys were already on their way to the pond.

"No one jumps in until I am out there to watch!" I yelled after them.

The older boys impatiently awaited my arrival to the pond to jump in. As soon as I arrived pondside with the youngest boys, jump in they did. Soon, they were laughing, swimming, and splashing. I settled into my chair with my eyes peeled on the water, counting kids, and smiling at the joy I could see in their faces.

There would be diving contests. Some displayed near perfect dives while others fell flat, literally flat, on their stomachs. "Ouches" could be heard by all of us as we related to the pain. It was short-lived, however, and the jumps continued.

After a while, the older boys would notice the younger ones playing in the sand pile that led into the shallow part of the pond. Before long, all five of them were digging in the sand. Today was the day they were going to make the best waterfall of the summer. One would start a large trench leading down the sand hill while another would create a large opening at the bottom to catch the rushing water. Others dug their own trenches, making sure the end of it joined with the main trench. They encouraged one another and offered suggestions. They even tried new ideas. A cave-in or two was bound to happen. After a collective groan, the rebuild would begin.

Soon, the path to the water was complete. The trenches were fully dug. The opening at the base was wide enough to adequately empty the water into the pond. All that was left was for the trenches to be filled with water. The kids grabbed their buckets and filled them with water. The little ones struggled to bring their buckets to the top, but each boy waited until all were in place for the big unveiling.

"It's ready, Mom! Here we go!" they yelled as they did a countdown and emptied their buckets into their trench. My face lit up with a smile. The sounds of ooo's and ahhh's made their way down the hill along with the water. The children watched with anticipation as the rushing water made its way through various side trenches. They cheered when the water returned to the main trench before swooshing out into the pond.

"Ya!" came the concerted yell as if indeed it was the best one they had ever built. After accessing some minor damage the water caused on its way down, the rebuild began. Once again, the best waterfall of the summer was about to be made.

Each time we went to the pond, the waterfall creation was the main source of entertainment. It did not matter if it was just my five boys or if friends had tagged along. It didn't matter their age or if some girls were in the mix. They would form a plan of action, and together, they worked hand-in-hand to build the best waterfall the summer had to offer.

As I watched them, I thought about how much we, adults, could be encouraged by them. The lesson on cooperation that I watched unfold before my eyes brought several thoughts to the surface.

I wondered if God had anything in mind for us to accomplish together.

I wondered if there was a community project that needed to be done by a group of people.

I wondered if there was a family who had a project in which they needed the help of others.

I wondered if there was something within our church that we could create to help others.

I wondered....

Teamwork is not a foreign idea to God. He speaks of it often in scripture. He lets us know we have a variety of gifts and talents we are to use to serve one another and teach one another about His Son, Jesus.

What team is God leading you to be a part of today? If we each commit to being part of a team and work on projects to glorify Him, just imagine the lives that will be changed. I hope the story of the waterfalls built by a group of children act as the reminder you need to encourage you to join together with others to accomplish the purposes God has in mind for you today.

Ponder & Pray

Who could you engage with today to accomplish something for God's purposes?

_____

_____

_____

_____

Heavenly Father, we thank you for the reminder that you desire for us to work together to accomplish your purposes. We ask you today to not only show us who it is that you desire for us to work alongside but also please show us what project it is that you would like to see us pursue with those people. We praise you for having the plan, giving it to us, and showing us how to move forward. Amen.

Day 24

The Unexpected

For the word of the Lord is right and true; he is faithful in all he does.

Psalm 33:4

With our hearts beating out of our chests, my boy-friend and I walked hand-in-hand into Meijer and headed to the aisle with the pregnancy tests. As 18-year-olds, this was far from the location we imagined we would find ourselves six months into our freshmen year of college.

After purchasing the test, we went to our vehicle and carefully read over the instructions. Seeing that the test was most accurate when taken in the early morning hours, we made a plan for me to be at his dorm before the sun rose the following day.

Sleep didn't come easily, if at all, for either of us that night. Laughs from roommates permeated the walls of our dorms as our minds searched the "what ifs" of the potential test results over and over in our brains. When morning arrived, I went into the bathroom and took the test before any of his roommates awoke. Carrying it back into his dorm room, we sat and stared at the piece of plastic that seemingly shape our future.

Positive. Immediately, panic flooded through us. But wait; there was a chance it could be wrong, right? There's an 800 number on the back of the box. Yes, of course. We may have done something wrong. Surely someone on the other end of the phoneline would know.

I sneaked out to the living room area of the dorm and took the heavy black phone off the wall. Carrying it around the corner to the bathroom, I dialed the number. The person on the other end did not ease any of my panic.

After the conversation, I tiptoed back into my boyfriend's bedroom. I searched his anxious and fear-filled eyes, hoping to make sense of what was happening. Was he ready to be a dad? He was just learning how to take care of himself. How was he going to take care of a baby and a wife? Was I ready to be a mom? I was barely keeping my head above water with my classes and being on the tennis team. Could I add a baby to that mix? While those questions swirled through my mind, one statement kept reverberating through my brain – I am pregnant.

My world shifted that day. All the future plans I had made for my life suddenly felt as if they were snatched out of my tightly held grip. I was lost. As my world spun out of control, I remember placing my hand on my tummy and saying, "Don't you worry little one. We're going to be alright." The words were spoken confidently; yet they were simultaneously spoken with words crying from the depths of my soul, "Lord, what am I going to do? What's next?"

You see, even in the midst of what I saw as an unknown future for myself and my baby, I also knew I served a faithful God. I had an understanding that the God I served was not going to desert me. He wasn't the type of God who would leave me hanging out on my own, even if I had strayed from Him. However, I knew this new path I was to embark upon was not going to be without its challenges. I knew there were soon to be difficult conversations with parents, painful decisions regarding my relationship with my boyfriend, and challenges concerning my education. Regardless, that never changed my view of my faithful God. I knew God would forgive me and would still love me. He would pick me up right where I was in that painful and confused state and set me back on course again. I knew He would be present with me when doubts of my ability to be a mom would attempt to smother me. I knew He would comfort me as I mourned the life I was leaving behind and the life I would never live. In hindsight, I would never choose my imagined life over the life that unfolded before me. I was fully convinced He would provide me with the direction and strength I would need as a young lady trying to make her way in a world that seemed impossible to navigate.

Life sure has some direction changes, doesn't it? Some of those changes are the results of decisions we made for ourselves. Others are thrown into our laps, almost as if to say, "Here, deal with this!" These directions changes can consume us as they fill us with doubt and fear.

Direction changes look differently for each of us, yet we all experience them at some point. For some, it's the spouse who isn't stepping up, so you feel you are leading your family alone. For others, you made some choices that went against God, and you are now dealing with the consequences. Some may be dealing with a sudden job loss or scary health diagnosis. Regardless of what your circumstances are today, I want to remind you that you are not alone. God will be faithful. It violates His character to be unfaithful. He can be trusted. He is here for you. The same faithful God who walked with me is available to walk with you. We serve a God who is in the midst of your situation. He desires to comfort you in your pain, forgive you of your mistakes, and walk with you as He directs the next steps of your journey.

No one cares more about you or the situation you are in than the God who created and loves you. He is faithful and will not leave your side. Will you choose to trust Him today with your situation?

In what area of your life are you struggling? Will you choose to trust God with it today?

_____

_____

_____

_____

Heavenly Father, I thank you for being a faithful God. I know trusting you should be easy as I understand you desire the best for me. But sometimes, it is difficult to let go of control and give it to you. I am choosing that today, Lord. I am trusting you in these specific areas of life. I thank you for providing the forgiveness, comfort, and companionship I need for the journey. Amen.

Day 25

Fearful Focus

Finally, brothers and sisters, whatever is true, whatever is noble,
whatever is right, whatever is pure, whatever is lovely, whatever is
admirable…if anything is excellent or praiseworthy…
think about such things.

Philippians 4:8

The sun had not yet risen over the Houston sky when our driver dropped my husband and I off at the MD Anderson Cancer Center that cool spring morning in 2015. I had a full day of blood work and imaging as well as an appointment with the surgeon. Tomorrow, I would undergo surgery to remove the cancer that had decided to make its home within the walls of my uterus.

Not long after my arrival, nausea and stomach pain took over my body. Could I possibly have a stomach virus the day before I was scheduled to get rid of this cancer? As the symptoms intensified and the trips to the restroom became more frequent, it was clear that yes, I was sick. After explaining my symptoms to those at the center, they worked to get me in quickly. The pain in my body only worsened; by now, I could barely make it to the restroom without assistance. However, delaying the test was out of the question. They wanted this MRI, and they were going to get it.

I had undergone many MRIs since my diagnosis. I knew I needed lay still for the entirety of the exam. I wondered how I was going to be able to lay on that cold table without moving and without needing to stop the test so I could run to the restroom.

My name was called. My condition caused the faces of those caring for me to turn to concern. Yet, they would see me through this. As I changed into my gown, I was certain I was going to collapse. The cool tile floor beneath my feet beckoned me. It begged me to lay down on it. The desire to curl up in a fetal position upon that floor took a strange type of resistance I had not met before this day. I needed to stay focused on the objective - get that MRI.

The man helped me onto the MRI table. The sterile, hard surface attempted to embrace me as my body shook. *Focus. You can do this. Focus.* My mind wanted to do anything but focus. My body wanted to be anywhere but on this table. The man explained that if I moved or interrupted the test, they would need to start it over. I understood. I also understood that it would take more than what I possessed within myself to make it through this test without rushing to the bathroom or curling into that fetal position that continued to tempt me. *Focus.*

What would I focus upon? God, are you there? I can barely think coherently, but I know you are the only one who can get me through this test. My focus will most certainly need to be on you. The machine began to move me inside the walls of the cylinder. As it did, music began to play but not just any music. To my surprise, a familiar song of promise by one of my favorite artists filled my ears. It was "Overcomer" by Mandisa. Yes, God was indeed here. My focus was on Him alone. My frail body and my fearful mind were fixed with laser focus on the Father who was in this cylinder with me. The Father who was walking this journey with me today. The Father who would walk with me in the days ahead as the cancer was removed from my body. He was the Father who made focus possible.

Focus is not always an easy mission to accomplish. The distractions are endless; ongoing temptations attempt to direct our focus elsewhere but especially away from God.

I wonder what you may be encountering today that takes more focus than you believe you have within yourself. Do you have a work deadline that is weighing you down but needs your focus? Do you have a spouse who is drifting further from you but needs more intentional attention from you? Do you have a child who calls for focus in a way that you feel you can't give right now? You may not have the ability to focus on what is on your plate today, but I guarantee if you change your focus to God, He will guide you. He will adjust the lens of whatever needs your focus today and equip you with the strength to zoom in on it in a way that would be impossible without His strength. You may not be able to focus like you need to, but with God, you can.

What do you need to do today to improve your ability to focus on God instead of the many distractions surrounding you?

_____

_____

_____

_____

Dear Lord Jesus, I need a mind-shift. Instead of being "me-focused," I need to be "you-focused." Please work on my heart by convicting me to look to you for guidance, peace, and strength. Gather my thoughts and bring them together in a way that focuses them on you instead of the issues surrounding me. My desire is to look only upon you with such focus that any distractions do not hinder my ability to see you. Amen.

Day 26

Jesus Loves Me

The Spirit of God has made me; the breath of
the Almighty gives me life.

Job 33:4

The pungent smells of the nursing home smacked us in the face when we walked through the doors. The aroma of the noon meal combined with cleaning solution was anything but pleasant. Nevertheless, as we made our way through the entry area, we smiled and said hello to the residents who looked up from their wheelchairs, hungry for more than the lunch sitting before them.

"Hi Grandpa!" we greeted as we walked into his room. He scooted himself up in his bed, smiled, and returned the greeting, always happy to see his grandchildren.

As the conversation began between our family members, I glanced around the room. The cement walls provided no warmth or comfort despite the meager attempt with the scattered pictures taped on them by the residents' families. Three other frail men shared the room with Grandpa. They laid in their beds sleeping or at least appearing to sleep. I wondered about the lives these men may have lived. It was as if stories of adventure, laughter, heartache, love, and loss were locked up inside bodies that could no longer share with us all that the prior years had held. I wondered if there were beautiful love stories hidden in their hearts. Perhaps some had fought in a war. Here I sat in their room, living in the freedom I often took for granted because of their sacrifice. Maybe they had great adventures of vacations with their families at a nearby lake or a distant mountain range. I bet they sat at the head of the table during a large family gathering and looked with pride at the children and grandchildren who surrounded them. Maybe they were lonely. Maybe they didn't have a family at all; they were heading into their last days in the same manner the years before them had been – alone.

I was suddenly jolted from my thoughts by a loud gargling sound from one of the men in the bed behind me. As I shifted in my chair to look, I smiled at a lady in the chair next to him. Her tiny body sat close to the bed with her hand stretched across the blanket, holding his hand. As the nurse made her way past me, she whispered in my ear, "His wife comes every day and sits with him, even though he never opens his eyes or talks."

Her statement spoke volumes, and I dismissed myself from Grandpa's bedside to pull up a chair next to the woman. Above his bed hung a small cross surrounded by some family photos. I began to talk to the woman and listened to her as she confirmed what the nurse had said. His unintelligible moans were frequent, coming several times each minute. From the reactions of his roommates and others who went in and out of the room, it was apparent the moaning had become as normal as the sounds of the nurses' chatter in the hallway.

It was after his wife shared about their family and her daily visits to sit with her husband that she disclosed the words that would forever be embedded in my heart. It was if she was waiting to save the best for last.

"I don't even know if my husband knows I'm here. He moans loudly around the clock. He doesn't speak…except for this. Whenever I sing 'Jesus Loves Me,' he joins right in and sings every word with me."

This frail body needed to be tended to for even the slightest needs. This man's moans filled the room all day, every day. Yet, this man would join his wife in singing "Jesus Loves Me" without missing a word.

As I left the nursing home that day, God impressed upon my heart two different lessons. The first was shown through the love and commitment of a woman to her husband. Her love was a literal display of the vow "in sickness and in health…til death do us part." May I strive to have that type of commitment in my own marriage.

The second lesson was brought to me as I left. The Holy Spirit washed over me, filling me with peace. He used this man to teach me that even in my darkest times, even when it seems I can't be reached, even when life seems to have gone on without me, God is still present. His love and His promises reach into the darkness, take hold of me, drawing me deeper into His presence, and remind me that He was there all the while.

I think most of us have gone through a time in our life where we feel lost and alone. We feel as if we are at the bottom of a deep pit with no exit in sight. Our situations may be different, but we all have experienced the walls closing in on us. The fear makes its way into our lives as we physically tremble. The anxiety presses down upon us as we gasp for air. And yet, this man's story shows us the fruit of what happens when we invest in filling our spirits with the Holy Spirit. When everything in his life was stripped away, what was left was a spirit that was still healthy and connected to his Savior.

What steps can we make in our lives to determine that when every part of our lives is stripped away, we are able to still have the comfort of the Spirit within us? A couple ideas that come to my mind are, for one, memorize God's Word. Psalm 119 says, "I have hidden your word in my heart that I might not sin against you." And in the New Testament, Jesus uses memorized scripture to make Satan flee from Him. The Word of God has power. When we take the time to memorize it, we are able to fill our spirits in a way that will keep us fueled even during those times when life is filled with darkness. Another idea is one that this man displayed when he sang "Jesus Loves Me." Worship music is powerful. Often times, it is filled with scripture.

Listen to it. Allow it to soak into the depths of your spirit, so it will surface once again during those dark moments.

Perhaps you can think of other ways to fill your spirit with His Spirit. Take some time with Jesus today and allow Him to minister to your heart. Connect with Him in a way that will reap rewards not only today but in the days ahead when you need Him most.

Ponder & Pray

Have you experienced the power of God's spirit during an especially difficult time? What can you do today to fill your spirit with all that God has to offer you?

_____

_____

_____

_____

Heavenly Father, thank you for ministering to me during the darkest of times. Please instill in my heart the importance of filling myself with your Word, your teachings, and your truths. I know that when I do these things, you will reside within my spirit in ways I may not fully understand. Yet, they are ways that will allow you to connect with my heart when I need it the most. Amen.

Day 27

Nudges to Move

My sheep listen to my voice; I know them, and they follow me. I give
them eternal life, and they shall never perish; no one will
snatch them out of my hand.

John 10:27-28

At nine months pregnant, my mind and body reached its limit after the long day. My husband looked at me knowingly; I had hit the wall. Exhaustion overtaking me, I settled into my recliner with a scoop of ice cream. I had eagerly waited for that ice cream all day. With the younger two children tucked into bed, I thought my mom duties were done for the night. I released a deep exhale and began to relax.

I yelled out to our two oldest boys, "Good night, guys! Love you! See you in the morning!" They were headed toward the steps to make their way to their rooms.

My fifteen-year-old's voice echoed from the staircase, "Mom! Aren't you coming down to tuck us in?"

"Come on, Mom!" shouted the ten-year-old.

My body tensed. My face grimaced. My mouth began to form the words, "not tonight, boys." After all, it had been a long day. I had just gotten comfortable or as comfortable as a woman who is nine months pregnant could possibly get. I had also tucked those boys in every night for the last ten and fifteen years. Surely a night without me wouldn't do permanent damage.

However, before the words "not tonight, boys" could escape my mouth, I wiggled my way to the edge of the chair. Hoisting my body out of it, I waddled down the steps.

There are those times in our lives when circumstances pop up that are a bit inconvenient. In truth, those types of things happen daily. Yet, I hope after a quick evaluation of those circumstances, we are able to discern which items may be inconvenient but are also worth the investment versus the items that are inconvenient and can be put on a back burner.

For a brief moment, my exhaustion took priority over my sons' needs. No, my sons' lives would not be significantly altered if I did not tuck them in that night. Yes, my sons could learn that sometimes Mom could say no. However, I felt that nudge. You know the nudge I mean.

It's that little push from God that gives us that boost we need to "get out of the chair." Tonight would not be the night I would say "no." After all, if my sons, who were ten and fifteen years old, were still asking for their mom to tuck them in, I most certainly would not turn down that opportunity.

By paying attention to the "nudge" God gave me that night, I was able to experience time with my sons that was more than worth the trip down the stairs. I was able to bless them with a mom who went the extra mile.

God has the ability to give us those "nudges" throughout the day. Often times, we are so consumed with the daily tasks around us, we brush off the "nudges." We convince ourselves they surely could be put off another day. Yet, very often the nudges from God are timely. Only He knows the exact moment when our friend is in need of a phone call. Only He is in tune with the financial needs of the neighbor who needs some grocery money. Only He knows the moment the young mom is feeling too overwhelmed to climb out of bed. With that said, the timing of His nudges is of utmost importance. They aren't intended to be put off for another time. When He speaks to our hearts and minds, it is because He sees a need and has the desire to use us to fill the need. I just think that is so cool! We serve a God who wants to use us to complete His purposes!

I wonder what nudge God would like to give you today? He has something in mind for you to accomplish for Him. I hope you will commit to listening, watching, and obeying the nudge. The nudge will give you the boost you need to "get out of the chair" and accomplish something that may seem inconvenient yet is very significant.

Ponder & Pray

What nudge is God giving you today and will you take action to obey it?

_____

_____

_____

_____

Heavenly Father, I thank you for the nudges you provide. I often get caught up in the routines of the day and forget to listen. I forget to pay attention to the needs of your people. Would you please open my heart today? Would you allow me to hear and to feel the nudges you give me? I thank you for turning "inconveniences" into blessings. Amen.

Day 28

Scrap the Plans

*"For my thoughts are not your thoughts, neither are your ways my
ways," declares the Lord.*

Isaiah 55:8

I had been dealing with an autoimmune issue with my
eye all week. Finally, the doctor's treatment appeared to
be working. I laid my head on my pillow that Friday night
and turned my thoughts to a lady's brunch I was speaking
at the next morning. My heart pounded with anticipation
and excitement for what the next day would hold. The
lady's brunch promised to be a wonderful time of visiting,
spiritual renewal, and of course, some delicious food.

However, the next morning, I felt dread and anxiety
overtake me. My eye had worsened overnight. As the pain,
redness, and swelling continued to grow, I knew I needed

to contact the doctor. He insisted I be seen right away. Looking at the clock, I was relieved to find it was still early enough for me to make my appointment and still get to the event on time.

With my husband driving, off we went for my appointment. Upon being seen, the doctor quickly informed me that I needed to see a specialist immediately. Unfortunately, this specialist was on the other side of town. My anxiety again heightened as I looked at the clock, wondering how I would be able to fit another appointment in and still make it back to the lady's event.

With tears streaming down my face, I contacted the church to let them know that there was a good possibility I wasn't going to make it. At that point, I wasn't sure if the concern over my eye was more intense or the disappointment at potentially missing the event. Either way, after an hour in the second office, I was an emotional and physical wreck. I could not imagine how I could possibly minister to the seventy ladies who were anticipating my arrival.

Heading out to the car after my appointment, I glanced at the clock. There was still time for me to make it to the event. My husband gently asked me if he should drive me home or to the church. I sat, unable to answer, as I wrestled with my options. After the happenings of the morning, I felt unequipped to go on with delivering the message to the group. I had been so excited to see these ladies and share with them the message God laid on my heart. Yet, I sat in that car, exhausted, and felt anything but worthy of sharing with them. I questioned my ability. I questioned my appearance. What could I possibly have to offer these women in my current condition? How could God possibly use me when I was so weary in mind, body, and spirit? "Lord, what do you want me to do?" I petitioned Him, asking for direction and guidance in my decision.

Suddenly, my Great Aunt Marney popped into my mind. This Godly woman, who I knew was praying for me at this very minute, would be at this event. And boy, could I use an Aunt Marney hug about now. Then, a church basement full of women popped into my head. Women laughing, praying, encouraging, and praising the Lord together. With these thoughts, I knew in my heart what my decision needed to be. I also knew I wouldn't be able to make it through my message without breaking down at some point and even shedding some tears.

When I shared my concern with my husband, he laughed and said, "What better place to break down and cry than in a room full of 70 God-loving women!" With that, he drove me to the church.

Upon my arrival at the church, I was greeted with smiles, encouragement, and yes, an Aunt Marney hug. I was able to deliver the message as well as find out my husband was correct - that group of women was the perfect place to shed a few tears.

The plans I had for that Saturday morning were thrown out the window as soon as I opened my eyes. Nevertheless, God still had His plans for the day. Instead of using an organized speaker, He used a scattered speaker. Instead of using a prompt speaker, He used one who showed up late. Instead of using a speaker with a "put-together" face, He used one with a red and swollen eye. Instead of using an energized and excited speaker, He used an exhausted and disheartened one. And most importantly, instead of just bringing my message to that group of ladies, He spoke a bigger message to me. One that reminded me that His plans are not hindered by my circumstances. One that taught me that His plans definitely don't need a person who thinks he or she has it all together. His plans involve taking the messed-up situations in life and putting them together to create something beautiful. His plans involve a group of ladies who arrive to be ministered to and leave having been the ministers. His plans involve a patient husband who loved his wife through a difficult situation. His plans are full of unexpected blessings. I realized I would choose His plans over my plans any day of the week.

God specializes in creating beauty from the ashes. Sometimes, those ashes are the unexpected circumstances in our well-planned lives. I wonder if you could take time to reflect today upon a time when life through you a curve-ball. Perhaps a time when you thought you would crumble because life was caving in on you. The anxiety and stress built up because you just couldn't figure out how the situation would end up with a "happy ending."

Unfortunately, those times in our lives are not once in a lifetime events. They are more likely to come on a regular basis. My hope is the next time you are experiencing one of those circumstances, you allow God to embrace you and set you on a new path. He will show you that He still has it under control if you allow Him to work within your situation. He is the master of taking the unexpected hiccups in your life and turning them into something far better than you could ask or imagine.

Ponder & Pray

When was the last time God changed your plans and how did it turn out for you?

_____

_____

_____

_____

Heavenly Father, I praise you for seeing the unseen, planning for the unplanned, and knowing the unknown. I thank you for taking the pieces of my life that seem unorganized, scattered, and painful and putting them together to create something that is glorifying to you. Please continue to remind me that the pieces of my life are in your hands and that you are creating something beautiful out of each of them. Amen.

Day 29

A Brother's Visit

Come near to God and he will come near to you.

James 4:8

Excited laughter buzzed through the house as the three younger boys planned for their older brother's visit from college.

"Mom! When will he get here?" they asked constantly.

When our son disclosed he would be coming home for a visit, the younger boys quickly set about planning all they would do for the weekend. Creating forts in the basement would certainly be on the list as would talking brother into sleeping inside said forts. Fishing, shooting baskets, and video games were certain to be blended with an abundance of conversation.

I was grateful these young brothers were so excited for their brother's arrival. My thoughts were interrupted by one of the boys yelling down the hallway, "He's here! He's home!"

The door flung open. The youngest bolted toward him, preparing for his customary "jump hug" greeting. He flew into the arms of his older brother who caught him just as the duffel bag was thrown to the ground.

The thirteen-year-old brother also made his way to the door but playing it a little cooler. They gave each other a high five and a "hey Bro," before laughing and joining together in an embrace.

As my college boy looked around for the last brother, we directed him downstairs. Brother number four, who had been calling and emailing his older brother as they counted down the days until this reunion, liked to keep his greetings a bit more private but with no less enthusiasm. As I followed him downstairs, I stood back and watched the exchange of a secret handshake and a hug. Little brother's eyes sparkled, telling this mom we were in for a great weekend together.

I don't recall all we did on that weekend. However, I do recall the unbridled joy of three little brothers anticipating a special time with their older brother. I remember the attentiveness my eighteen-year-old son gave by spending time playing and listening to his younger brothers.

One reason this memory is embedded in my heart is that this was not an unusual scene. This eighteen-year-old brother had not been gone to college for months. He did not live hours away. In fact, he had come home every weekend since college began, and he lived less than an hour away. The best part of the story is the excitement they each had for spending time with one another when the reality was they frequently spent time together. It was, and continues to be, a mom's answer to prayer.

Isn't it a wonderful feeling when someone desires to see us so much the person is counting down the days, hours, and minutes? I love that! I also love that it reminds me of how much our Savior desires to spend time with each one of us. As a parent, I pray daily for the relationships my five sons have with one another. The prayer sure doesn't stop there. The bigger, more important prayer is that they have a desire to build a relationship with their Savior. It is a prayer that they would hunger for Him and be eager to spend time with Him. I pray they long for the moments when they sit at His feet and soak in His Word. I pray they pour out their own prayers to Him.

God created us with relationships in mind. We are designed for relationships with others and a relationship with Him. He loves it when His people are anticipating their time with one another. He cherishes the fact that we make one another a priority, especially when we show His love to others through intentionally building those relationships.

In addition to creating us for one another, He ultimately created us for a relationship with Him. Oh, how He desires for us to have a hunger to spend time with Him. Remember how my younger sons kept asking about the time, bursting with excitement about their big brother coming through the door? When we have that same excitement about spending time with our Heavenly Father, it brings Him such joy. He loves it when we allow Him to walk with us through our everyday schedules. He eagerly anticipates the times when we sit with Him and set aside our busy schedule to meet. He will even "look" for us in the basement, if necessary, to greet us and continue to pour into the relationship.

Today, I pray you will look at the day ahead and make your relationships a priority. Invest in the lives of the people around you by setting aside time to build and enjoy those relationships. May you also invite Jesus to walk with you through the day, so you can converse with Him along the way. Take some moments out for just the two of you where you can spend time listening and sharing. I guarantee you will eagerly anticipate your next opportunity to sit down together.

How will you adapt your schedule to ensure you spend time strengthening your relationship with others and Jesus?

_____

_____

_____

_____

Dear Lord, I am thankful for the relationships you have placed in my life. I look forward to continuing to strengthen them by spending time investing in the people you have placed in my life. I thank you for my relationship with you. Life gets so busy, and I admittedly do not make my relationship with you a priority. Please forgive me for that. I commit to take time for you daily in prayer and bible reading. I look forward to knowing you more fully and strengthening our relationship into all that you intend it to be. Amen.

Day 30

Grandma's Cookies

Dear friends, since God so loved us, we also ought to love one another.

1 John 4:11

The clanging of pots and pans could be heard from the kitchen. The smells of turkey and Grandma's stuffing wafted through the house, reminding us that the coming meal was going to be delicious. The boys grabbed chairs from the garage to set around the table while the girls scampered around setting the tables with everything needed to devour the eagerly awaited food. Children gathered on the living room floor with their toys strewn about. They played with cousins they'd excitedly anticipated seeing since they said good-bye after the last holiday meal.

Despite all the hustle, everyone had one thing on their mind. When was Grandma Zee going to get there?

Nothing was quite complete until she arrived with her famous chocolate no-bake cookies.

Suddenly, the door swung open, and there she stood with a plateful of the most delicious cookies on the planet.

"Grandma's here!" one of the children hollered.

"Did she bring her cookies?" another chimed in as they made a b-line for the door toward Grandma.

The sounds of pots and pans quickly subsided. The boys paused bringing in the chairs. The girls stopped setting the table. The children put down their toys and ran to the door.

Soon, Grandma was barricaded in the doorway, greeting each person by the unique nicknames she created for each one. Grandma had a special way about her. Her greeting was more than just a greeting. She intentionally looked you in the eye and spoke with such love. Her words made their way into the depth of every heart. It was if you were the only person in the room with her.

Grandma slowly inched her way into the house, taking in the group that stood before her. Each person vied for her attention; we were drawn to her like metal to a magnet.

Suddenly, someone exclaimed, "Grandma, do you have your cookies?" Other voices joined in saying, "Do you, Grandma? Did you bring them?" With a smile beaming from her face, she lifted her plate of cookies toward the ceiling. Cheers could be heard echoing throughout the house.

What made Grandma's cookies so special? Did she use a specific type of cocoa? Did she have a secret ingredient? No, that wasn't at all what made Grandma Zee's cookies so special. The answer was quite simple, and also something no one else could replicate. It was Grandma. She was the ingredient that made her cookies "so special."

It wasn't the sugar; it was her smile that would brighten any room. It wasn't the cocoa; it was her company and her ability to make everyone feel special. It wasn't a list of ingredients; it was a listening ear that perked up with the voices of her grandchildren. It was purely and simply the love of a grandma, who seemed to sparkle all the more brightly when she was surrounded by the ones who adored her.

I wonder if you have had a "Grandma Zee" in your life. Have you had someone whose very presence made you feel cherished and valued? Perhaps this person had his or her arrival tied into something like cookies, a little toy, or trinket. Maybe this person had a little saying that would connect his or her heart to yours.

Just as the grandchildren felt seen, loved, and valued by Grandma, God asks each of us to reach out to others. We are to pour His love on all those we come into contact. He longs for others to see Him because of the love they see in us. Could you consider today how you can play a part in sharing His love to someone by serving that individual in a way that would honor the Lord?

Ponder & Pray

How could you make someone feel loved and valued today?

_____

_____

_____

_____

Heavenly Father, I thank you for the many ways you show your love to me but most specifically, by sending your son, Jesus to this earth. My desire is to love others as Jesus does. Please bring to my mind someone today who specifically needs to be reminded of the love you and I have for them. Thank you for giving me the opportunity to share your love with others. Amen.

Day 31

The Wave Good-bye

There is a time for everything, and a season for every activity
under the heavens.

Ecclesiastes 3:1

Summer was ending, and the last vehicle made its way out of the driveway. My hand slowly rose for the "good-bye wave." Tears formed in my eyes, and soon made their escape down my cheeks. My husband wrapped his arms around me, knowing the evening would be difficult. Even the days ahead would leave their mark as sadness weaved its way through our home.

You see, my emotions are pretty predictable this time of year. My personality shifts, and I become more withdrawn. I get a little short with my husband. I grow quiet. It's not a new thing. In fact, it's happened ever since my children were little, and I knew summer was ending. I sort of slide into a little depression. I don't want to let go of all that made our summer so special. I want to hold onto it so tightly, hoping that will make it last just a little longer. Yet, each year, it somehow slips through my tightly clenched fists, and the fall schedule begins. Years later, with children grown and grandchildren now in the mix, I continue to hold on with clenched fist. I long to enjoy the laughs around the bonfire; the swims at the pond; the sounds of the guitar playing in the bedroom; and the banging of furniture during wrestling matches just a little while longer. I don't want to say good-bye. I surely don't want to begin the process of letting go of the past and embracing the future. It seems so final and so permanent.

I share my sadness with my husband, and he offers as much comfort and help as he can. However, I have learned to bare my heart before God. Every single year, I share with Him my lack of zeal for transitioning from summer to fall. Each time, He faithfully reminds me of the importance of the transition and yes, even the joy to be found in the transition. Oh, what I would miss out on in my life if there weren't these transitions. How I would miss seeing God work in the lives of my family if they didn't move from one chapter to the next.

Our God is so good to allow us the opportunity to grow and to transition from one chapter to the next. He is so good to allow us to create memories in one chapter while building anticipation for what the next chapter may hold. He is so good to allow us to take all that we learn - the good decisions and the bad - and to carry those lessons into the next chapter. Thank you, Lord, for walking with us through these times of transition. Thank you for extending grace to us as we mourn the season we are leaving behind. However, you also remind us of the growth and opportunities that come with the new chapters you have for each one of us.

I wonder what transition God has you going through right now. Like me, it could be the transitions brought on by a different stage of life for your family. Perhaps you are dealing with the needs of elderly parents or a scary health diagnosis that demand adjustments in your life. Maybe your job is forcing a transition. Whether welcome or not, the change can be challenging. Regardless of the transitions and whether the transitions are desired or not, I pray you will take His hand and walk this transition with Him. Allow Him to put people in your path who will make each day a new adventure filled with much love and hope. Allow yourself to feel excited about the many new memories on the horizon. I pray you are reminded that He has a plan for you and for your loved ones. This transition does not take Him by surprise. He had a plan in place for it long before you were even a thought in someone's mind. The plan includes this transition, but it also includes a beautiful new chapter.

Please remember that without turning the page to the new chapter, you will leave the remainder of the story untold. It's a good story. Go ahead, take the leap, and turn that page, even if you need to leave a tear-soaked page behind.

How are you feeling about the transitions in your life? Are you allowing God to show you what His plans are for this new season of your life?

_____

_____

_____

_____

Dear Lord, you are well aware that times of transition are difficult for me. I like to hold on to traditions and the past. As a result, I allow them to rule in my heart. I have trouble trusting you for what comes next. Please pour your comfort upon me as I let go of the past. Fill me with anticipation for what you have for my future. Amen.

Day 32

Uniquely Created

I praise you because I am fearfully and wonderfully made. Your works are wonderful, I know that full well.

Psalm 139:14

As we walked around the beautiful South Carolina mall area, the gentle noise of the fountain could be heard amidst the chatter of people visiting on the brightly colored benches. Lush green grass was perfectly manicured. The paths on which we walked were lined with vibrant foliage that was unfamiliar to my Michigan eyes.

It was while my six-year-old granddaughter and I were skipping along one of these paths that something caught my eye. I paused to take a closer look. There in the midst of the green plants, all sporting their variety of shades and shapes, was one brilliantly colored red leaf. I couldn't help but admire the beauty of this leaf that stood in stark contrast to the hearty, green leaves.

My granddaughter bent over to see what had my attention and quickly noticed the red leaf. After a satisfactory examination, she smiled and continued to skip down the street. Still smiling, she explained to me that it's important to be different. She went on to share that we should be happy when we are different and exclaimed, "Grandma, let's look for more things that are different on our walk today! We don't want everything to be the same."

"You're so very right!" I chuckled.

That little red leaf became the topic of conversation and provided the perfect opportunity to spend a couple minutes talking about the importance of our uniqueness. Not only should we acknowledge the different ways God creates, but we should also celebrate these differences. God made some tall, some short, some thin, some thick, some black, and some white. The list goes on and on.

Unlike the beautiful, red leaf, some differences do not seem lovely or captivating. Middle school and early high school were rough years for me. I vividly remember physically developing much later than other girls and feeling inadequate about my body. I also recall being referred to as "Black Teeth" by a classmate. He laughed with his friends from the back of the classroom, discussing the discoloration of my teeth. I was far from feeling any desire to celebrate my slower rate of maturation or the color of my teeth. Can you relate?

I think most of us would agree that we have parts of ourselves we would rather not embrace. Parts we question and silently wish were not a part of our characteristics at all. We may find ourselves comparing our appearance with the appearance of others. We may look at the talents of others and convince ourselves we have nothing to offer. We criticize ourselves in ways we would never criticize others. We question our very value. It's during those times of comparison we need to be reminded of what my granddaughter brought up that day. There is beauty in our differences and value in our diversity. The God-given opportunity to share in our distinct differences is a gift we should treasure. When there's temptation to fit in with our surroundings, we need to instead be excited about the opportunity to stand out. When the temptation is there to blend in with the background, we need to instead be bold. God's desire is for us to rejoice in who we are and who He created us to be.

Remember the "Black Teeth" nickname? It recently made its way back to me in a most unexpected manner. A grown man, who was a stranger to me, commented on one of my social media videos. He said, "I wish God would give you new teeth. I'm sorry for you because of the color of yours!" Upon reading the comment, I immediately heard the voice of my classmate back in high school. I was hurt and shocked that such a thing was being written about me. I had a choice to make. I could stew in my pain and allow those words to take root, or I could remember what my Heavenly Father says about me and meditate on His thoughts towards me. I chose the second option. I paused and prayed. I plucked out the "seed" of those words and stopped them from growing inside my heart again. I understood they were destructive words, and I had no need to create space for them in my life. I made a conscious decision to smile a big, teeth-showing smile in the midst of something that was intended for harm.

What part of yourself do you pick apart as you long to change the way you were created? It's so tempting to allow the negative thoughts to enter our minds and beat us up until we feel worthless. But, please hear me. God doesn't intend for those thoughts to be planted in your heart. He doesn't want them to establish roots and to gain strength. His desire is for you to acknowledge, and embrace the unique ways He created you.

Whether it's your physical appearance, your personality traits, or your gifts and talents that are "different" from others, it is reason to celebrate. What a boring world it would be if we were all the same. God was very intentional about the unique ways He created us, and His plan was certainly not for us to hide those differences. His plan is for us to celebrate them and to use them to change the world.

I hope as you go about your day today you will ignore the temptation to fit into the molds others have created. Instead, take some time to "skip down the street" as you recognize God created you to be the red in the midst of the greens in the world today.

Ponder & Pray

What is something about yourself that has been difficult for you to accept because it is "different"? How will you begin today by celebrating and embracing that difference?

_____

_____

_____

_____

Heavenly Father, I am often tempted to look and behave like those around me. Yet, I know your desire is for me to be the unique person that you created me to be. I thank you and praise you for creating me with purpose and for intentionally sprinkling in such special characteristics that can't be found in any other person in the world. Show me how to not only acknowledge the unique way you created me but to take time to celebrate it. Thank you for making me…me! Amen.

Day 33

Decisions! Decisions!

No temptation has overtaken you except what is common to mankind. And God is faithful; he will not let you be tempted beyond what you can bear. But when you are tempted, he will also provide a way out so that you can endure it.

1 Corinthians 10:13

As my middle school aged son threw items into his duffel bag for his overnight stay at a friend's house, we chatted about the fun he would have with his friends at this small party. His younger brothers gathered around, wishing they could get in on something fun like a sleep over at a friend's house. Ever the big brother, my son explained they needed to be a little bit older to spend the night somewhere. To lessen the disappointment, he promised he would be home in the morning to play with them.

161

"Mom?" he asked. "May I take a couple of our movies over to their house to watch?" This was back when VHS tapes were still the option of choice for family movies.

"Of course. Grab a couple good ones." I responded, knowing this was a great opportunity to bring up the movie choices that would be acceptable to watch at a friend's home.

I shared with him that some families had movies in their homes we didn't find appropriate. We talked about some of the movie ratings as well as what those movies might contain that would be unacceptable to view. During this discussion, one particular movie title came up. It was very popular and had just been released on video. We both knew it was not one he should watch. We discussed some ways he could quietly exit the room if the movie was played. Assured he was prepared to handle the situation, he gave me a hug and left for his friend's home, hoping he wouldn't need that exit strategy.

The next day arrived, and our son was dropped back off at home. Duffel bag in hand, he bounced into the kitchen. With a smirk and a raise of his eyebrows, he said, "Mom! You will never guess what movie the guys put in the VCR to watch last night!"

Oh, I had my guess alright.

"Yup, Mom. The exact movie we talked about me not watching."

He explained how after they had all played games, they settled down for a movie. The host brought out the movie we had specifically discussed as being inappropriate. He could feel the peer pressure as he listened to all the guys make remarks about how pumped they were to watch this movie. He had to make a decision.

Glancing up, he made eye contact with one of his friends. Observing the expression on my son's face, the friend gave him a "what's up" sort of look. Our son leaned toward him and said, "I need to leave the room. I'm not allowed to watch this movie."

With that, he got up and left the room. However, he wasn't alone; another friend followed him out. The two of them enjoyed playing a game together instead of watching the movie.

Temptations. They lurk around every corner. They appeal to our sense and appear appetizing and attractive. They beg for our attention and plead with us to take part in their illusive pleasures. Temptation sneaks up on us in various forms. It could be joining in on gossip during a break at work, submitting to the urge to verbally tear down a spouse, spending too much time on social media, and eating or drinking excessively. For a middle school boy, it came by way of watching an inappropriate movie.

As with all things, there is a cost to giving into temptation; it is not worth the price. They are harmful to others and ultimately, to our relationship with Jesus. Choosing to surrender to a temptation causes us to sin. Sin is something that gets between us and God, putting a wedge in our relationship. All is not lost, however. There is always an out or an exit plan. Our scripture verse from 1 Corinthians 10:13 says, "No temptation has overtaken you except what is common to mankind. And God is faithful; he will not let you be tempted beyond what you can bear. But when you are tempted, he will also provide a way out so that you can endure it." This verse is confirmation for us that although temptations will continue to press upon us, God does provide a way out of them through His Son, Jesus. When Jesus walked on this earth, He too was tempted to sin. And yet, He alone remains the only one who has not succumbed to sin. It is through His strength that we can also turn away from temptations. When we make the decision to lean into Him instead of leaning into the pressure of the temptation, He will give us the strength to turn from the temptation that is threatening to cause us to sin. It will not be comfortable, nor will it be popular. You may even be harassed for standing up against the temptation. However, the opposite may happen. Like in my son's situation, your determination to stand against the temptation may provide another the courage to stand as well.

Is there a particular temptation calling out to you today? I hope as the next temptation makes its way into your life, you choose to stand against it. I hope you choose the option that honors Jesus, your family, and yourself. I guarantee when you do, you will feel empowered and strengthened as God pours His affirmation into you.

Ponder & Pray

What temptation is difficult for you to conqueror? What steps could you put in place today to help you overcome it?

_____

_____

_____

_____

Lord Jesus, I know you are aware that the world is filled with temptation, and you know the many I deal with daily. Thank you for promising a way out of the temptations I face. I ask you for forgiveness during those times when I give into the temptations, and I ask for you to convict my spirit and pour out your strength upon me to stand up against those temptations. Please replace them with something glorifying to you. Amen.

Day 34

Flowers by Mom

*The L*ord *God took the man and put him in the garden of Eden to*
work it and take care of it.

Genesis 2:15

We moved into our new, ranch-style, brick home during the bitter cold month of February. We waited impatiently for the Michigan sun to break through and bring us spring days. With the flurry of activity that was typical of our family of six, soon to be seven, time did fly. Before we knew it, we found ourselves with not only spring but a new baby boy to add to our family.

Time management with now five boys proved to be quite challenging for me. While the outside of our home was pleasant enough, I dreamed of seeing colorful flowers mixed in with the bushes. However, I was far from being able to plant the flowers I silently wished lined the front of our home because my postpartum body just wasn't at a place yet to accomplish this dream. My struggles did not go unnoticed by my mom. In addition to the care she gave the boys, she always made time to check on her baby, me. Now, my mom had a passion for planting flowers and creating the most beautiful flower beds in the world (that's my vote, anyway). Since spring was finally here, she was busily planning and planting her flower beds. Knowing how much it would mean to me, my mother offered to plant flowers for us as well.

I remember gathering the three younger children to head out to the front yard with my mom as the older two ran to the backyard to shoot some baskets. The youngest rested in an infant seat placed in the grass. The other two little ones played in the dirt, helping to prepare it for the flowers Grandma would soon be planting. Having just had a baby, I wasn't going to be much help. Mom positioned a chair in the perfect spot for me to see the kids as well as the planting process she was about to undertake.

The older boys took a break from shooting hoops to unload flats of flowers from her trunk. They resumed playing, and she began putting her plan into action. She pulled weeds, dug holes, and placed plants in the dirt. I sat amazed as she seemed to do so with such ease. She even kept two playful boys, who insisted on helping, entertained.

After many trips inside for diaper changes, water breaks, and walks around the yard, the flower planting project was complete. We all stepped back and soaked in the meticulous way mom had created a paradise right there in our yard. Bright red petunias waved in the breeze as stark yellow marigolds stood strong. Dashes of purples and whites against the backdrop of green bushes created a glimpse of heaven.

"Yay, Grandma!" one tiny voice yelled out. Another, too young to create many words, jumped up and down clapping. The excitement rang to the back of the yard, and the two older boys came running over to see what the cheering was about.

Upon looking at the garden, they too were amazed. Going over to hug Grandma, they both greeted, "Thank you, Grandma! Wow, this is amazing!"

We all stood, side-by-side, admiring the gift my mom had just given us.

It is such a blessing when someone invests in us. The gift is especially appreciated when they pay extra attention to details. It makes us feel good inside and valued as we soak in the fact they found us important enough to spend their time blessing us.

First John 3:1 says, "How great is the love the Father has lavished on us, that we should be called children of God!" Just as my mom lavished me, her daughter, with her love by planting those flowers, God loves you so much that he refers to you as His own child. I just love that truth! He knows you intimately and understands every part of you. He knows exactly what details of your life need some extra care and additional love. He knows how to make your sometimes messed up life beautiful again. He can reach inside your heart and pull the weeds of fear and anxiety. He can prepare the ground by softening your heart toward those who anger you. He can plant fresh and beautiful plants of boldness and relief.

Then, you can stand with Him, side-by-side, and tell Him, "Wow, God, your work is amazing!"

Ponder & Pray

When do you feel most loved by another person? By God?

_____

_____

_____

_____

Dear Lord, I thank you for loving me so deeply. You care for each of my needs, even before I know what they may be. My desire is to experience your love more each day, so I am then able to share it with others. Amen.

Day 35

God's All Around Me

But the Advocate, the Holy Spirit, whom the Father will send in my name, will teach you all things and will remind you of everything I have said to you.

John 14:26

The day had been long, and I was finally getting my two youngest to bed. My then six-year-old was away at an evening church camp with some friends. Maybe, when our friends dropped him off, I could scoot him to bed quickly as well.

Before too long, our six-year-old came walking, well more like bouncing, through the door. This wasn't going as I anticipated. He had way too much energy. His blonde hair bobbed up and down as he ran over to me. "Mom, you should hear this story the man told at camp tonight!" he exclaimed.

Summoning what little energy I had left to sound cheerful, I said, "Really, what did he have to say?" I hoped this would be a short one.

Thankfully, my son did not pick up on my fatigue as he launched into the story the speaker shared. I heard about how God had healed this man after a serious fall. He told me every detail of the story as if the story was embedded into his mind.

"God did a miracle just like he did in the Bible, Mom! Really! This man wasn't supposed to be able to walk ever again, and he was walking and talking with us!" he continued.

Realizing this was no ordinary experience for my son, I asked him to pause. We should tell Daddy the story too. I followed him as he ran down the hallway and jumped up on our bed. He made himself comfortable before beginning the story again for Daddy.

When he had completed the story of healing, he paused. As he looked into our eyes intently, he explained that the man asked if anyone would like to pray and invite Jesus into their hearts. Our son stopped his story as he attempted to keep the tears from trickling down his cheeks. Daddy explained that he had tears many times, especially when he hears great things that God is doing.

With the blessing to allow the tears to flow, he did just that. He shared how he and other children made their way to the front of the room to pray and ask Jesus into their hearts.

Then, his big blue eyes locked with ours as he said, "It's just that God was all around. I could feel him all around me, everywhere in the room."

Our hearts were full. We had just witnessed two beautiful miracles ourselves. The first was our son's testimony that he began a relationship with Jesus. The second was that he had experienced what it felt like to have the Holy Spirit fill a room with His presence.

My fatigue had been replaced with gratitude. I was able to lay my head on my pillow that night with several reminders from our loving Savior. Not only did He teach me that it is always worth it to take the time to listen to our children, He also reminded me of a couple important lessons. First, we still serve a God of miracles, "just like in the Bible." Second, the Holy Spirit is present and evident.

It makes me wonder what the world could be like if we walked around really soaking in His presence. If we listened to His Spirit, allowing Him to lead our steps and touch the deepest parts of our hearts. It is easy to disregard daily connections and circumstances as coincidences. We very easily fall into the temptation of giving "medicine" all the credit for a healing instead of calling it a miracle. Yet, I believe God is in the midst of every situation. I believe His desire is to speak to us through His Holy Spirit. Sometimes, that is a little voice we may brush off as our conscience. Other times, it may come through scripture or through another person delivering a message God wants us to hear. Our part as the receiver of these messages is so important. Often times, this is the way God calls us to serve others.

Other times, it is how He provides comfort or wisdom to us when we are in need.

Today, I hope you will open your heart and spiritual ears in such a way as to really feel and hear what the Lord has to say to you. Wouldn't it be wonderful if we chose to live in such a way that we could say, "God is all around. I can feel him all around me, everywhere!"

Ponder & Pray

Have you experienced a time when you felt the Holy Spirit "all around" you? What were the circumstances?

_____

_____

_____

_____

Dear Lord, I know I fall into the trap of thinking that miracles are for Bible days only. I ask for your forgiveness for those thoughts. Even in that trapped way of thinking, I also know your spirit is here and dwelling in my midst. I want to experience you more fully and to have the excitement of saying I can feel you "all around" me! Please come upon me today and remind me of how very real you are. Amen.

Day 36

Needing Grandpa

*The LORD is close to the brokenhearted and saves
those who are crushed in spirit.*

Psalm 34:18

With five sons, I have come to expect bumps, bruises, and even, some tears. Sometimes, tears resulted when one of the brothers "stole" a toy. Other times, it was not being able to do something they wanted to do. More often than not, it had to do with the fact that when five brothers want to play together, things get rough. The living room turns into a wrestling ring. The nerf hoops hanging from the door create the chance for hard fouls. The list of potential pain opportunities is truly endless.

On one particular day, my work was stopped short from an ear-piercing scream. I say scream because this wasn't a normal cry. This was a scream of pain that I had come to recognize as the sound of my youngest, who was five years old at the time. Had this same scream happened years earlier with my oldest son, I may have already dialed 911 as I tripped over myself and tried to reach the living room at breakneck speed. Since it was my youngest, I had been here before. I quickly, but calmly, made my way out to the scene of the accident.

As I approached, his scream got louder. His brothers covered their ears. Thankfully, I found myself relieved at the site of him. He stood in the middle of the floor jumping up and down, which I took as a good sign. After all, there must be no broken bones if he was jumping up and down. However, his screaming continued. "My teeth are falling out of my head! Ouch! They're all gonna fall out!"

While I looked over his teeth and attempted to calm his trembling body, his brothers explained that he attempted to do a flip off the couch. The flip apparently came to a sudden halt when after only making it partially around, he jammed his knee into his mouth as he hit the floor.

He continued to cry and explain to me that his teeth were loose and falling out of his mouth. After careful examination, I reassured him that his teeth were intact. Though it hurt, he was going to be alright. Hugging him once again through his sobs, I thought I had done enough to convince him that he was not going to be a toothless five-year-old. Apparently, my examine and words were not enough.

"Ggggooo get Grandpa!" he yelled breathlessly in my face. "I need Grandpa to look at me."

My dad happened to be in the basement working, so big brother ran downstairs to get him. My son explained to Grandpa that he needed to hurry and look at his little brother's teeth right away.

Making his way to his grandson, Grandpa leaned down and asked my little guy what had happened. After the explanation, he took a look into his mouth and patted him on the head. "Yup, looks like you're going to be ok," he said satisfactorily.

For some reason, that was all the convincing my son needed that day. Grandpa went back downstairs to work. My little guy swept his hand across his face to wipe his tears, took a deep breath, and went on with his playing. I stood there wondering, *Didn't I just tell him the same thing Grandpa did?*

We all need a Grandpa in our lives. You know, the special person we run to when life knocks our teeth out. The same person we can run to for comfort or look to for the pat on the head. They reassure us that things are going to be alright. For whatever reason, when that special person gives us the pat on the head, we really do believe that everything is going to be alright.

Are you going through a difficult time today? As an adult, I am fairly certain your pain doesn't come from a knee to the teeth. The pain from rejection, mental health circumstances, or loneliness are more likely for us adults. However, they are not any less painful than a knee to the mouth. It is during those times we need to rely on the comfort of a "grandpa." I hope you can rest in knowing our Heavenly Father is that ultimate Comforter for you.

He desires to listen to your cries on those days when life is "knocking your teeth out." He desires to "pat you on the head," reassuring you that each day brings with it a new beginning. He desires to show you that you will be alright and that He's with you every moment of the journey.

Ponder & Pray

What are you going through today that creates the need for you to be comforted by your Heavenly Father?

_____

_____

_____

_____

Heavenly Father, often times, my life is challenging. I have those days where I feel like I have been kicked in the teeth. Yet, your scripture reminds me you are close to the brokenhearted. It reminds me that you are here for me and always available to comfort me, even on my most difficult days. Please provide for me your comfort today. Allow me to visualize what it feels like to be in your arms, resting in the knowledge of how very much you love and care for me. I thank you for that comfort, Lord. Amen.

Day 37

Defrosting Godzilla

For the wages of sin is death, but the gift of God is eternal life in
Christ Jesus our Lord.

Romans 6:23

It was a blustery winter afternoon. My husband and three children were glad to be heading into the house after the long day away. Our plan was to get unbundled and settle in for the night. The evening agenda might even include a family video or a game.

As we unbundled ourselves, one of the boys headed straight to the bathroom. However, he came frantically running back out to us. "Godzilla is dead! I think he's dead!" he yelled.

With a glance at my husband, we both knew this night was not going to go as planned. Godzilla was an iguana our oldest son received for his birthday several years prior. Although the lizard was quite small when he arrived, he had since outgrown his glass tank. He now lived as a "free-range" lizard in our bathroom. Comforting our boys after the loss of their favorite pet would not be an easy task.

Once inside the bathroom, we quickly realized what had happened. Godzilla had climbed onto the windowsill. That normally was not a problem except for the fact our window was in need of a repair. The glass on the inside pane was broken. Godzilla had crawled through the hole and spent the day between the inside windowpane and the storm window. You see, Godzilla loved sunlight. The highlight of his days was basking on the windowsills as the sun shone through. Today, however, his desire for the sun may have cost him his life.

Although Godzilla was perfectly healthy when he climbed through the hole in the window that morning, he appeared to have made his last climb. A cold breeze blew through the cracks all morning and developed a thin layer of frost on the inside glass panel. Godzilla went from a healthy lizard to a frozen lizard as he sat between the windowpanes. The question remained: could Godzilla be saved? My husband and I certainly hoped so; but as we stared at his lifeless body, the odds were not in his favor.

When we opened the window and retrieved Godzilla, he didn't move a muscle. Unlike his normal, wiggly self, he was as stiff as a board. Tears streamed down the boys' faces. In an effort to offer some hope, my husband mentioned to the boys that Godzilla was a coldblooded animal. There was a small chance he would come back to life if we heated him back up. I'm still not sure if my husband totally believed this would work or if he was buying time before we had to have the boys say good-bye to their beloved pet. Either way, we were going to give it a try.

The five of us squeezed inside our small bathroom. Dad placed Godzilla on the floor in front of the heat vent. I turned the heat up so the air would begin blowing. There we all huddled around Godzilla, looking for any sign of life. The minutes went slowly by. "I don't think anything's happening, Dad," one of the boys said. As Dad looked into my eyes, he responded, "Well, he was pretty frozen. Let's give him some more time." The boys took turns gently rubbing their finger along Godzilla's back while we continued to sit on the floor. We continued to wait. Hope was nearly gone when, suddenly, one of the boys saw it.

"I think I just saw his eye move!"

His eye? Really? Could it be? Seriously? We all tucked in closer to Godzilla and stared at his eyes. As one of the boys reached out to touch his head, Godzilla slowly moved it again! Yes! We all saw it with our own eyes this time! The eyelid on the right side, closest to the blowing heat, actually moved! Was it possible he was thawing? Although smiling, my husband and I were hesitant to appear too hopeful because this little creature still had at least twenty-three more inches to thaw.

Minutes later, one of the boys noticed another movement. "His toe just moved!" Not soon after, his leg began to move. Yes, indeed! Not only were his eyelids opening and closing, his legs were starting to move too. While we all acknowledged the pain this creature must feel going through this thawing process, we were still able to reach for the hope that he was truly on his way to a full recovery.

By now, over an hour had passed. Godzilla was progressing nicely. He was soon able to slowly and carefully walk forward, dragging his stiff tail behind him.

"What about his tail?" one of the boys asked. "It's furthest from his heart so it's going to take a little longer," responded older brother, obviously having some knowledge of how the whole reptile anatomy functions. Big brother was correct. After watching Godzilla walk a bit more, his tail loosened up and was soon swishing behind him like normal. Bedtime had finally rolled around for the boys. Thankfully, they able to rest that night, secure in knowing that Godzilla had definitely come back to life.

The analogies between Godzilla and our spiritual life abound. The one that touches my heart today is the comparison between our lives and the situation in which Godzilla found himself on that blustery winter day.

Have you noticed that we can easily be caught up in situations that have the appearance of pleasure only to discover the situation leads to problems and heartaches? Sin is like that. It can appear grand, luxurious, sexy, fun, and comforting. It's all things that we, as human beings, find appealing. Let's go back and visualize how the sun was shining through that bathroom window. Its warmth created a most inviting location for a reptile. The bathtub or carpet paled in comparison to the windowpane. It seemed like such a wonderful idea.

Oh, how similar we can be to Godzilla. We take a look at something appealing but fail to see the sin because the disguise is so enticing. Temptation may come in the form of the extra food or drink we shouldn't consume. Maybe it's the flirting we did with someone who isn't ours. Perhaps it is being a part of the group that is tearing someone else down. Perhaps it is viewing the websites we all need to be avoiding. Maybe it is the small lie we told. Maybe it's the shortcut we took while working on our finances. The list goes on. The sun in the windowsill looks different for each of us. However, the truth is, we all spend time on the windowsill. We climb up to the sin. Before we know it, the sin so entirely consumes us. We are unable to remove ourselves. We become "frozen" in our sin.

This is where God enters. He is the Father who sent His Son to remove us from the windowsill. He provides the exit plan from the sin that has us frozen. Because it is usually difficult to leave sin behind, sometimes even painful, He will hold us as we go through the process of making the needed transitions. He will comfort us as we go through the pain that often is a result of our sin. Once we turn away, He turns us loose for a new life. We get a new start as we "come back to life" through Him.

Ponder & Pray

Is there a sin you need to take to the Lord? Are you willing to allow Him to forgive and heal you from it?

_____

_____

_____

_____

Heavenly Father, we recognize we are sinful people. We get caught up in sin that appears glamorous but soon traps us. We thank you for reaching down and pulling us out of that sin. Your forgiveness allows us to have a fresh start because of the salvation you offer through your Son, Jesus. Amen.

Day 38

Calling the Father

See what great love the Father has lavished on us, that we should be
called children of God! And that is what we are!

1 John 3:1

The sound of my phone startled me out of a sound sleep at 6:00 am. Seeing my son's name on the screen, my mind immediately went to that dark place. This son was away at college and normally in bed at this time. Was there an accident? Is he sick? I imagined all the worst-case scenarios. It's amazing how many thoughts can go through our minds within a split second.

"What's wrong? Are you alright?" I asked, answering the phone. I soon learned that he hadn't gone to sleep yet because of a terrible pain in his tooth. Pretty sure it was a tooth infection, he needed to head home so we could take a trip to the dentist. I completely agreed that this would be the best course of action. Throughout the brief conversation, my son apologized three times for calling me so early and waking me up. As sweet as it was that he was apologizing, my momma heart and mind was so thankful he called. *Thank you for not sitting through another minute of pain without letting me know what you are going through. Thank you for telling me how you feel, so I can take the steps needed to get you the proper care. Thank you for loving me enough to include me in your difficulty.*

As I thought about that phone conversation, God touched my heart. It was as if He was saying to me, "Misty, that's how I feel about you calling out to me." I considered this and was reminded of the great love our Heavenly Father has for us. First John 3:1 reminds us of this love when it says, "See what great love the Father has lavished on us, that we should be called children of God!" What joy it is to be reminded that our God loves us so much, He calls us His children! I am a child of the Living God! He says so! It means that whatever I am going through, His heart is right there with me.

I know it is sometimes tempting to think we need not bother God with the small issues in our lives. We may wait to go to Him until the problems build up and we have nowhere else to turn. Instead, He wants us to go to Him right away. He doesn't need us to wait until our lives are in such disarray that we can't see a way out. He wants to hear from us right from the beginning. He desires to communicate with us on a daily basis. He wants us to include Him in the "small stuff," just as He wants us to include Him in the "big stuff." When I think of how thankful I was when my son called out to me, I am quickly reminded of my Heavenly Father, who desires that type of relationship with us. We may call on Him at any time of day, even in the wee hours of the morning. What's even more amazing is we do not have to worry about waking Him from sleep. Our God never slumbers. He waits with a listening ear all day long.

What is it in your life today that you should be sharing with your Heavenly Father? You will not need to apologize for calling on Him regardless of the topic or the time of day. Are you sitting in a struggling marriage? Call Him. Did you receive devastating health news about yourself or someone you love? Call Him. Do you have a child who is turning from your family and God? Call Him. Are you struggling to pay the bills or have a job loss? Call Him.

I guarantee that when you call on Him, He will say, "Thank you for calling me, my Son or my Daughter. Thank you for not sitting through another minute of your pain without letting me know what you're going through. Thank you for telling me how you feel, so I can take the steps needed to care for you properly. Thank you for loving me enough to include me in your difficulty. Thank you, Sweet Child."

I pray that, today, you will pause right now and talk to your Heavenly Father. We serve a God who loves us as His children. Knowing how much I love my children, I cannot even imagine the perfect love our Heavenly Father has for us, His children.

Ponder & Pray

Is there something in your life that you are struggling to share with God? Are you willing to turn that over to Him today?

_____

_____

_____

_____

Heavenly Father, I thank you for loving me more than I can imagine. For loving me as your child. Today, I commit to sharing with you the challenges I encounter. I commit to pouring my heart out to you, allowing you to walk through each and every day with me. Amen.

Day 39

Every Frog Matters

But because of his great love for us, God, who is rich in mercy, made us alive with Christ even when we were dead in transgressions - it is by grace you have been saved.

Ephesians 2:4-5

Frogs. They may seem like insignificant little amphibians to most of us, and others may find them utterly disgusting. As a mom of five sons, I can assure you that frogs have always been anything but insignificant in the Cramer household. As children, my boys couldn't go for a walk without keeping an eye out for the tiny critters. To this day, as grown young men, frogs still excite them. If they are blessed enough to see a tree-frog planted against our living room window, the adrenaline rushes, and the boys gather around to get a closer look at the intriguing little, green creature.

On one warm spring day, my young son asked to go on a walk with Grandpa and myself. We were all well aware of the unpredictable nature of Michigan weather during the spring. The unusually warm day did not represent what it had been the day prior, and it certainly wasn't a forecast of what was to come the following day. With that knowledge, we determined to seize the moment. Making our way down our country road with the warmth of the sunshine hitting our backs, we headed out for our journey.

It didn't take my son long to realize that we weren't the only ones who were coming out to enjoy the exceptionally warm day. As we walked, so many frogs hopped out of their homes to enjoy the sun warmed asphalt. Like any good spring day, the heat was not to last. The temperatures started dropping as the day progressed. My son's excitement at all the frogs quickly turned to horror as he realized these frogs were getting trapped. My dad and I realized our walk was going to turn into a rescue mission as my little guy quickly went into "frog catching mode."

You see, with the sun starting to set, the asphalt had begun to cool. These once lively frogs were not moving well on the cooling road. The creatures that normally leaped high and jumped great distances without issue now looked as if they were in slow motion as they attempted to jump across the road. Most of these frogs were crossing the road to make it back to their homes in the ditch-bank. However, they were stuck in the middle of the road, paralyzed from the now cold asphalt. The cold wasn't their only enemy that evening. Let's just say when an oncoming car and a frog meet on the road, the frog does not win. Nevertheless, my son was determined to save these frogs from their dreadful predicament.

As we walked, I pointed out frogs in need of assistance. "There's one on that side. Oh, there's one here by my foot. Watch out, Grandpa, don't step on that one in front of you." My frog rescuer ran from side to side, grabbing the unsuspecting frogs. With a smile covering his face, he would carry it off the road and put it in the ditch where it would be safe. This frog saving adventure went on for close to a mile. My son ran as quickly as he could from one frog to another, attempting to save as many as he could before a car drove past.

Some may have watched my son as he attempted to save as many frogs as he could and shook their heads at the futility of this undertaking. After all, he was hardly making a dent in the frog population, so why even try to save any of them? Others may say that the frogs should be left to fend for themselves. After all, they did get themselves into this predicament.

Yet, if those people were to ask my son, he would be quick to let them know the truth. He would say that even if there are lots of frogs, he thinks every frog matters. It would be sad to let even one of them die. He would then probably ask, "Haven't you ever done anything dumb?" He would continue to explain that just because the frogs did something dumb, like hop onto the road, it wasn't a reason to let them get squished by a car.

Grace isn't deserved. Second chances aren't always earned. Yet, there isn't one of us who lives a life without a blemish or many blemishes for that matter. We serve a God who is willing to chase us down whatever road we are traveling, scoop us up in His hands, and rescue us from the death that would certainly be waiting for us if it were not for His rescue mission.

You probably won't find me on the road saving frogs; I will leave that to my little frog rescuer. However, I am thankful I serve a God who believes I'm worth saving. I'm thankful that even in the midst of my "dumb decisions," I'm never too far gone for Him to reach. I praise Him because although I am only a small part of this big world, He loves ME, and I matter to Him!

It is easy to allow thoughts of inadequacy and worthlessness to creep into our hearts and minds. We often beat ourselves up because we convince ourselves we don't measure up to others. We speak harshly to ourselves when we don't hit a goal we were attempting to attain. We find ourselves hopeless when we fall into the same sin again and again. Can you relate? I want to remind you today, we serve a God who believes we are more than adequate. He believes you are worthy. He believes this so much He went to the cross and died for you. Thankfully, the story doesn't end there. He came to life again to redeem you and provide you with hope and a new life. His desire isn't for you to spend time with negative self-talk. His desire is for you to find freedom in Him by allowing Him to pick you up off that road and take you to a place where you can flourish.

Today, I hope you will join me in praising Him as you come to know you are worth saving. You are never too far from His reach either. Although you may think you are only one small part in this big world, to Him, you are worth everything. YOU are loved, and you matter to Him!

Ponder & Pray

Have you allowed God to rescue you? If you haven't, are you ready to do that today?

_____

_____

_____

_____

Heavenly Father, some days I question that I am a person worth saving. I see the mistakes I make, and I am reminded of poor decisions I have made. Yet today, I am reminded of who You say I am. My heart is beyond thankful, knowing that although I am a sinner, I am made new because of your mercy and your love for me. Thank you, Lord, for loving me and believing that I am worth saving. Amen.

Day 40

Finger Forgiveness

If we confess our sins, he is faithful and just and will forgive us our sins and purify us from all unrighteousness.

1 John 1:9

This is a bittersweet day for me as I write the last devotion for this book. In fact, my heart pounded as I asked God to direct me to which devotion should be the final one to leave with you. His answer was quick and clear: Finger Forgiveness. I believe it is because this short devotion embodies the ultimate message God has for you. It is the message of His unconditional love and forgiveness. Thank you for taking this journey with me. Would you please open your heart with me as you read this last devotion? My prayer is that God uses it to fully cement His truth into your heart today.

I was packing up the last items of the night and preparing to lock the door behind me when a scream made its way from the church parking lot into the building. It was a scream of pain, and I quickly realized it came from my middle son. I dropped my things, handed my youngest child off to someone standing nearby, and bolted outside. There, I found one son screaming in pain as his older brother looked on with tears flowing down his cheeks. "I'm sorry. I'm sorry," he said over and over.

The van door had been accidentally closed on his fingers. It was evident by the scene who had closed the door. I hastily climbed in the van to find we needed to go to the hospital for stitches.

After finding other people to care for the remaining brothers, my husband drove us to the hospital. I sat in the backseat with our son doing my best to comfort him. His screaming continued as his injured hand laid in his lap and the other gripped my hand.

Suddenly, the screaming stopped. "Mom, he said he was sorry. And he asked me to forgive him. I will always forgive him. Cuz he's my brother." As abruptly as the screaming stopped, it began again. Yet, this six-year-old child had paused just long enough for God to use him to teach us all a lesson on unconditional love and forgiveness.

As we wrap up this book, I pray today you are aware of the Savior who always loves you and forgives you. There's no need for begging. There's no need for wondering. Just as our son had no wavering in the love and forgiveness he offered "cuz he's my brother," the love and forgiveness of our Lord is freely given, plain and simple, because you are His child. No questions asked. It's as if He hung from the cross, writhing in pain, paused, and said, "Father, I will always love and forgive because that is my child."

If you have not surrendered your life to Jesus, I pray you will do that today before you close this book. All you need to do it acknowledge Him as the Son of God, ask Him for forgiveness, and accept Him into your heart as Lord of your life. My heart, and more importantly, the heart of Jesus, wants nothing more today than for you to become a part of the family of God.

Ponder & Pray

Have you asked Jesus for forgiveness and become a part of the family of God? Would you like to do that today?

_____

_____

_____

_____

Dear Heavenly Father, I thank you for unconditionally loving me as your Child. I thank you for sending your son, Jesus, to earth and to die on the cross for my sins. His sacrifice offers your forgiveness. I praise you because He conquered death by rising from the dead in three days. As a result, I have the opportunity for eternal life. I acknowledge that I am a sinner; I do many things out of your will. I lay those things at your feet and ask your forgiveness. Please come into my life and embed yourself into my heart. I make the decision today to accept your free gift of salvation and commit to become a follower of you. Thank you for giving me the opportunity for abundant life on this earth and eternal life some day in heaven. I give you all the glory, honor, and praise as I celebrate today by becoming part of your family. Amen.

If you are already a follower of Jesus, I pray you will pause today before you close the book to ask God what the next step in the relationship is for you. As with every relationship, it takes time and effort to strengthen it. Perhaps it's time for you to commit to a more regular prayer time. Maybe it's time for you to read the Bible more consistently. Maybe God is calling you to serve Him in a new way. Enjoy spending time searching for what He has next for you. Would you pray with me the following prayer as we close up this devotional?

Ponder & Pray

What new commitment will you make today to
strengthen your relationship with Jesus?

_____

_____

_____

_____

Heavenly Father, I thank you for unconditionally loving me. I praise you for the relationship I have with you. My heart's desire is to take this relationship a step further. As I pause for a moment, please place on my heart what new commitment you would like to see me make for our relationship. I make the following commitment:

_____

Please prompt me each day to keep this commitment to you and give me the hunger to continue to grow my relationship with you. Amen.

Thank you for joining me on this 40-day journey. You were prayed for as I was writing this book. I will continue to pray for you as you move forward in whatever God has in store for you now. With that said, I would love to celebrate with you if you prayed either of the prayers listed in today's devotion. Please shoot me a message along with any prayer praises and requests you may want to pass on to me. I would find it an honor to walk with you on your faith journey and pray for you specifically along the way.

May God bless you, hold you close, and guide you as you experience the "everyday" moments He places on your path.

URGENT PLEA!

Thank You For Reading <u>The Every Day God</u>!

I really appreciate all of your feedback, and

I love hearing what you have to say.

I need your input to make the next version of this

book and my future books better.

Please head to your Amazon account and rate my book.

Thank you! This means a great deal to me!

Misty

Also, I would love to connect with you! I'd love to pray for you! I'd love to
hear about your story! I'd just love to get to know you more!

Facebook: Misty Cramer, Author & Speaker

Instagram: @mistydawncramer

Email: mistycramer18@gmail.com

AS A BONUS, RECEIVE THE FREE DOWNLOADABLE GUIDE:

"5 Steps to Walking with God through Everyday Moments"

Receive it today at

mistycramer.com

Acknowledgements

In addition to those to whom this book is dedicated, I am blessed to have many people in my corner, covering me in their prayers throughout this process. I'd like to take a brief minute to express my deepest gratitude to each of you.

My first "official" steps on writing this manuscript began with my attendance at the Speak Up Conference with Carol Kent and her team. The entire team at the conference has blessed me in countless ways. I specifically thank Gene and Carol Kent, Bonnie Emmorey, Sandi Banks, Bruce Martin, and Cheri Cowell for pouring into me in ways you probably didn't even know. That's the cool thing about it; it just came naturally for you. Yet, your affirming words and encouragement to keep moving forward provided me with what I needed to continue toward the goal of writing this book. I will forever be one of the biggest fans of the Speak Up Conference and the team; thank you.

The Speak Up Conference led me to the She Writes for Him Tribe (SWFH) at Redemption Press. Thank you, Athena Holtz and team, for providing a safe place to grow. The friendships that developed within this Tribe are ones I will always treasure. Thank you, SWFH Tribe!

Also, through my Speak Up connection, I met Matt Emmorey, who led me to Self-Publishing School (SPS). SPS turned out to be my home for publishing this book. My SPS Coach, Andrew Biernat, became one of my biggest cheerleaders. He continues to guide me each step of the way on this foreign journey. He somehow made the challenging road of publishing into a fun adventure. I can't mention SPS without mentioning those I met with weekly in the Writing Room. You guys all rock! Keeping one another accountable and cheering one another on has been one of my favorite parts of this journey. I came to look forward to those morning and afternoon sessions with each of you. Keep on going! You will soon hold your book in your hands. Thank you SPS team and SPS authors!

Thank you to my editor and new friend, Eleanor Kersey. What a delight it has been to get to know you and what an honor to have your handprint on my book. I pray the very best for you as you continue to move forward with your editing business.

I couldn't do this book without my Prayer Intercessory Team. Each of you have prayed me through this journey, and I thank you so very much. When I emailed you to let you know I was headed to the keyboard, I knew your prayers were being said and heard. I could feel them. Thank you for taking this prayer assignment seriously. I am beyond blessed to have you in my life.

Oh, my Imagine 320 Ladies, you know who you are. You're the ones who have been in my Bunk House for the past many months on Thursday nights. Together, we have studied God's Word, shared our hearts, cried, laughed, ate, and prayed for one another. You're my people. You're my friends. You each have a special place in my heart. You have walked with me throughout this process and have had a close-up view at my week-to-week progress and setbacks. Thank you for being a part of the community God called to keep me moving forward. I love you all.

Thank you to my incredible family, immediate and beyond. You have each served me in different ways since I began to put this book together: prayers, cards, texts, financial help, gift cards, meals, and so much more. Thank you for the individual ways you have been the power behind this process. It has meant so much to me to have you as part of this journey. I love you all. For my siblings, you will find your own stories written within the pages of this book as I share about our lives together. I hope you enjoy the path into the past as you relive some of those memories with me. I thank God for placing you in my life. I am grateful we are part of one another's stories, on paper and in person. I love and treasure you so very much.

Meet the Author & Her Family

Misty Cramer grew up on a farm in rural Michigan, only a couple miles from where she raised her own family and currently lives with her husband, Todd. Writing a book never seemed too far-fetched for her since her love for writing began when she was young. Whether it was journal writing in the top bunk bed of her childhood home or winning a writing contest in sixth grade, her love for the written word has always been evident. Soon after her youngest son was born, she accepted a columnist position for a local newspaper. There, she wrote a monthly submission not unlike the ones in this book. Encouragement from her family, friends, and readers continued to leave a lingering desire to put her words into book form. Thus, the dream became a reality with The Every Day God.

In addition to her writing, Misty has been involved in full-time youth, family, and marriage ministry for over thirty years. Whether she leads a women's bible study or takes a couple hundred students on a spring break trip, her passion is to show others the love Jesus has for them.

Today, Misty continues to be involved with youth ministry through Youth for Christ while also ministering to women through her business, Imagine 320, which she began in 2021. Through Imagine 320, she connects with women from around the country, coming alongside them in prayer, coaching, teaching, and speaking. She speaks at various events, from MOPS to Women's Retreats to Family Camp Events as well as Marriage Retreats with her husband, Todd.

As an "empty nester," Misty enjoys making the rounds visiting her five sons and their families. Spending time with her family has always been, and will remain, her favorite way to spend the day. Whether it's a good game of pickleball or a boardgame, competition flares within the Cramer Home. You will find Misty in the middle of it, loving every second.

To complete the book, Misty thought you may find joy in putting some faces to the family mentioned in the book. Enjoy!

"The Cramer Boys": Stephen, Taylor, Zachary, Harrison, and Micah

Misty, husband Todd, and their sons Stephen, Taylor, Zachary, Harrison and Micah

Misty and Todd

Misty and granddaughters, Jada and Layla

Misty, Todd, and Misty's parents, Larry and Vickie

The Cramer Family

Made in United States
Troutdale, OR
11/15/2023

14596974R00137